I0116565

Another at the Pool:

When Healing Doesn't Come

Jennie Martin

Copyright © 2002, 2013 by Jennie P. Martin
All rights reserved.

Published by Sapphire Visions
Printed in the United States of America
ISBN: 0692279393

All scripture quotations are taken from
The *New King James Version*.
Copyright © 1979, 1980, 1982, Thomas
Nelson Publishers, Inc.. All rights reserved.

Copies of this book may be ordered at
www.sapphirevisions.com.

Sapphire Visions
Farmington, AR

To My Family

ACKNOWLEDGEMENTS

I am deeply grateful to many who provided assistance with the completion of this manuscript:

Billy Randles, for invaluable assistance with insights and clarity of thought

Rebecca Randles, for editing and sound advice

My parents, Melvin and Sylvia Steele, for their unconditional support and encouragement

My brother, Mel Steele, for his sacrifice for my health

Steve and Susan Rives, for their technical expertise

And especially for my husband, Mike, who has exhibited continual patience and love.

I would also like to give special thanks to St. Joseph Health Center of Kansas City, Missouri, Dr. John Ervin, and Dr. John Fried for their excellent care.

Table of Contents

Chapter One:

"Them" Is Me

"Girls, I thought I asked you to quiet down. You're going to wake the dead!" It was Mom, impatiently shouting out the back screen door at my sister, Ruth, and me. Once again we had gotten carried away, belting out one of the many hymns we had learned in church.

Although Ruth couldn't have been more than eight, and I not more than six at the time, our passion for evangelism was unstoppable. We deliberately climbed to the top of our swing set at every opportunity that hot summer to coax anyone who might be listening into committing her life to Christ. We didn't understand how Mom could possibly squelch our enthusiasm. It never occurred to me until I was older that our squeaky voices probably only amused our neighbors, if it didn't annoy them altogether.

My view of Christ was simple and straightforward then. Living for Jesus meant sharing His love, and I attempted to do just that. Without question I accepted what I was taught, as I never had a reason to doubt those time-tested truths. Even at a young age I tried to live out the commands of the Lord, however comical my efforts may have been. Christianity was a way of life for our family.

In those simpler days I never thought much about sickness and death. The few funerals I had attended as a child were for older people whom I assumed had already lived a full life. Of course I knew that young adults, even children, got sick and died. But that was so distant from my own experience that the few people I had heard about were the silent "them." I was healthy and never for a moment thought that would ever change. I had not yet come to the time in my life when my beliefs would come face to face with a severe chronic illness that would test them to the limit.

I have since learned that the "them" is me. I also believe that at some point that is true for each of us. At some time in our lives, ugly issues surface that we never dreamed could touch us or our loved ones. Natural disasters, divorce, job loss, a wayward child, sickness and death – any of these or a host of other calamities may befall us, despite our best efforts to avoid them.

This book is for anyone who has suffered such a loss. Especially, this book is for those for whom deliverance has not come and for those who love and minister to such individuals. These pages contain my emotional diary, including my bitter struggle with depression and anger; a scouring of scripture in an attempt to find answers; and most importantly, a look at how my relationship with Christ changed - when healing didn't come. My prayer is that you will be blessed as you read along, by examining your own walk with God.

Family Living

I grew up in a household of seven with three sisters and one brother. We didn't have much money but we didn't feel poor. We had two parents who loved the Lord and their family. Dad was the first one from his family to graduate from high school. Amazingly, he even managed to make it through college and get his master's degree – with a wife and kids.

No matter how busy Dad was with his job or studies or how tired Mom got was taking care of a husband and a house full of young children, church was a definite priority. Saturday night rituals prepared us for the big day. There was laundry to do and the careful laying out of Bibles and Sunday School lesson books in preparation for the busy morning.

Dad's task was to polish our shoes. While we slept our little Sunday shoes sat on an old newspaper beside his seemingly giant ones, left out to dry till morning. I really enjoyed Saturday suppers when we usually ate grilled cheese sandwiches and a weekly treat of 7-Up. Sunday morning breakfasts were always rushed so we got to enjoy chocolate donuts and milk.

We could be seen faithfully filing into church three times a week: twice on Sunday and again on Wednesday night. Dad was later ordained as a deacon in our Southern Baptist church in Kansas City, Missouri, where I was born. He and Mom were very involved and busy teaching a class more often than not.

At six years of age I was convinced that I was called to be a missionary to Africa. After all, I had been taught that only boys grew up to be preachers or deacons. But excited reasoning told me that girls could grow up to be missionaries; and I had heard there was a considerable need for them in Africa.

I made my own profession of faith in Christ when I was seven. A karate expert had demonstrated his abilities in a parking lot across the street from our church as a prelude to our area revival. The impending question of the hour was, "If you died tonight, where would you go?" I knew then that I wanted the salvation and security that Jesus alone could offer. I told Mom I wanted to go to the front to pray and accept Christ into my heart. That night Dad walked up the aisle with me and before the night was over I had become a Christian.

We eventually moved to the small town of Nevada, Missouri, where in the footsteps of my parents I began teaching Sunday School at sixteen. I remained active in my local church right up until I graduated from high school.

College Changes

Following my preset agenda, I enrolled at Southwest Baptist University in Bolivar, Missouri, a private college of then approximately 1600 students. Two of my closest friends and I set out almost immediately to impact our world with the foolproof methods we had learned. Possibly the most dramatic illustration of this would be our befriending a sophomore guy with a bad drug habit. Surely a heart-felt prayer would solve the problem.

We gathered a modest group of concerned friends and conducted a prayer service outside our dorm amidst the fallen leaves of a starry night. How dismayed we were to discover that it would in fact require many more prayers and much heartache before our friend's life was once again on the right track. How simplistic was my faith at this point in life.

I participated actively in speech and debate, as I had in high school. It consumed much of my time. I invaded the library in the evenings and attended tournaments on weekends. I spent any spare time with friends, dated some, and went to most of the social functions. During my sophomore year a friend and I even took up jogging. Essentially, I lived a normal college life.

My relationship with God began to change during this period. Suddenly there was no one to wake me up every Sunday morning to go to church. What began as an eager attempt to solve the crises experienced by those around me with a "quick-fix" prayer evolved into a sense of frustration.

I still regularly attended church on Sunday mornings, but my level of involvement declined. The bond with my Savior gradually tapered into a superficiality that became frighteningly comfortable. How I wish my faith had not been so mechanical when illness ultimately struck.

Halfway through my second year of college strange things started happening to my body, things that shouldn't happen to a nineteen-year-old. My joints stiffened. I developed severe back pain and chronic fatigue. In fact, I began dozing off during the day. I had little control over this overwhelming urge to sleep. That spring semester I fell asleep in virtually every class, every day.

I would wake up with a jolt in English class or in Biology, only to find scrawls of ink on my paper that were invariably illegible, so I borrowed class notes from my friends. Once I fell asleep about halfway through a Government test. I woke up shortly before the hour was over and hurriedly completed the multiple-choice test, not even stopping to read the questions. I melted inside as I trudged back to my dorm room, only to fall asleep again.

I tried various methods of camouflaging my in-class naps. I discovered that if I positioned the book and notes on my desk just right, and tilted my head towards them propped up on one elbow, I could look pretty studious – and sleep at the same time. I tried hard to pay attention to the lectures and always kept a pen in hand, poised to write on top of my strategically placed notebook.

This technique worked tremendously well, until I started to fall out of my chair in Algebra. My body began to sway and I was barely able to catch myself in time to avoid becoming a laughingstock. Thanks to my friends and a good-natured professor, a plot developed to take advantage of my irresistible urge to sleep.

They brought a rope and actually planned to tie me to my chair. Then I would be awakened with a question from the teacher. Fortunately, I was told about the scheme and foiled their well-laid plans by uncovering the hidden rope. The whole escapade provided much needed amusement for everyone involved. But inside I was petrified.

I confided my real fears to Denise, who insisted I go to a local physician. The early diagnosis of my excruciating back pain assured me that I only had underdeveloped back muscles. But that did not account for the chronic sleepiness or the joint pain. Even placing a stiff board under my dorm bed for extra support did nothing to relieve the anguish.

Soon I realized that something was terribly wrong. Still I hesitated to go to another doctor because I was afraid to find out what the real problem was. In the end, not knowing became even more frightening. I forced myself to admit that I could no longer hide behind a well-placed notebook or the laughter of good friends.

The next doctor, our old family practitioner, tested me for arthritis. When that evaluation returned negative he assured me I was merely sleeping in awkward positions, which was why I woke up with such stiff joints. He also diagnosed me as a borderline diabetic and prescribed a special diet and some medication.

Summer Struggles

This diagnosis was only the tip of the iceberg and barely hinted at what lay beneath the surface. But leaving it at this caused excessive damage, partially because it led me to believe I had been imagining everything.

I returned to my routine, living as normal a life as was possible at that point. But as I had secretly suspected would happen, my health only continued to deteriorate. My joints stiffened even more, making it extremely difficult to walk or to grasp an object. All the simple tasks I had taken for granted now represented monumental efforts on my part.

In spite of these growing complications I had an intense desire to maintain my independence, not to let an unknown illness slow me down. I awoke early one summer morning and sat down to write a letter. Everyone else was asleep and the house was quiet.

I stacked the paper close to me, propped my feet up on the coffee table and began to compose the letter in my head. I picked up the pen to remove the cap so I could transfer those thoughts onto the paper. But no matter how hard I tried, the pen cap would not come off. I was devastated. If

I could no longer do even these simple tasks on my own, then my plight only looked more and more bleak. Still the doctor continued to insist that nothing was wrong with my joints. I felt helpless.

Silently crying, I woke up my brother and sheepishly asked him to uncap my pen. He took one look at my tear-stained eyes and knew I really needed help. Without complaining he pulled the cap off and rolled back over to sleep. Slowly and painfully I crept back to the couch, more determined than ever that the letter I had sat down to compose would get done right then and there.

My condition grew worse until one morning later that summer I woke up around two a.m. in excruciating pain, worse than any I had endured thus far. I literally could not move at all. My body refused to turn in either direction. I panicked and called for help; but because of the noise of fans in the house, no one heard me. I lay in utter agony until my mother began stirring at 6:00.

"Mom, I need you," I cried out feebly. Thankfully she heard me and helped me get dressed. I insisted on being moved to the couch, away from the tormentor my bed had become as it held me captive for hours. I was scared. I knew the doctor was wrong, but I also didn't know what the answers were.

Later that day I went to yet another physician. He was also unable to discover the source of my problem, but he did prescribe medication to alleviate the pain. I was put on prednisone, an addictive steroid, and started feeling good again. It disguised my pain for a time. Then suddenly the bottom dropped out from under me. I was out of pills due to a mistake on the prescription.

I later learned that prednisone is a drug that has to be reduced gradually or it can cause damage to the body. Your body becomes used to the dosage and relies on it. Going from forty milligrams a day for a week to nothing made me feel worse than I had before I started.

I plummeted to an all-time low. No one seemed to be able to tell me what was really wrong, much less help me eliminate the trouble so I could get on with my life. I was frustrated with the pain but more so with being in the dark about the war my body was waging on itself.

For perhaps the first time in my life I truly did not know how to pray. At this point a big part of me still denied that anything could possibly be seriously awry. So although I prayed for God to help, I never really struggled with the questions that came later. I lived in a tunnel of sorts, seeing only what I wanted to see and keeping God at a distance.

Living with the Diagnosis

Out of desperation I soon returned to my family doctor. At his wit's end, he admitted me to the hospital for further testing. I was eventually diagnosed by a rheumatologist as having Systemic Lupus Erythematosus (called SLE or lupus for short), a disease that affects the body's immune system.

I later learned that lupus is known as an autoimmune illness. *Auto* means self. So an autoimmune disease is one that directs itself against the body's own tissue. Under normal conditions, when harmful bacteria invade the body, antibodies, which are protective substances in the blood, are developed to help fight off the infection.

With lupus, antibodies may be formed without the presence of foreign substances like bacteria. These new *autoantibodies* attack the body's own tissues. This in turn can cause inflammation and injury to body tissues and organs.

Although lupus can potentially assault any of the major organ systems of the body, its organ of choice is usually the kidney. The disease is characterized by alternate periods of remission and exacerbation. It is incurable and shortens a person's expected lifespan. So at nineteen years of age I had to confront a nightmare. I had an illness that could not be cured and that could ultimately kill me.

I returned to school for my junior year and basically tried to ignore the lupus. I took my medicines unobtrusively and attempted to conceal my overwhelming fatigue. But there were definite telltale signs I could not hide. The prednisone, which was re-prescribed, made my face round and fat, giving me the appearance of a chipmunk.

I also lost some hair due to my mix of medications. It started coming out in handfuls whenever I washed or combed it. This frightened me because I was unprepared for it and did not know it was a possibility.

My close friends on the speech and debate squad realized that my rapidly thinning hair was a major source of embarrassment to me. Their proposed remedy was to provide levity to an otherwise grave situation.

"Billy, not again! How could you?" was often heard in a loud whisper as quiet snickers erupted into noisy laughter. While I slept on the van one of my good friends on the squad had twisted strands of hair on my head so they stood at attention. And once again I had forgotten to check my hair before entering the restaurant where we had stopped for a quick bite to eat.

I had been given a small exercise book and what looked like a giant, wide blue rubber band to help stretch out the joints and muscles. I faithfully performed my prescribed exercises on a daily basis, even at speech tournaments. Billy invariably tried to steal my exercise band. Then he would dangle it just out of reach or use it to snap people. It was a relief to be able to laugh about those things.

To further prove my energy level was unchanged I made sure I was part of the forensic league pillow fights, a must at every tournament. This was my unauthorized aerobics, which frequently left me so tired I hyperventilated.

Even then I did not think the illness was all that significant. After all, I had gotten it under control, hadn't I? I was back at school and feeling pretty good, able to carry on almost like normal. So what if I got tired more easily and my physical appearance was affected? I told myself that I generally masked those things quite well.

The First Big Downhill Slide

Unfortunately this charade did not last long. The spring semester of my junior year I got very sick, very fast. The lupus hit full force and with more than an ordinary vengeance. The backs of my hands became spotted, my voice got weak and my body withered until it was too much of a chore to get out of bed for the day. I lay in bed long after my sister, Karen, and our suitemates had left for class.

The building hosting my afternoon class was only yards away from my dorm. Still I could not walk that far, much less the decidedly farther distance to the cafeteria. Sometimes in the early afternoon I donned my long blue robe and slowly groped my way down the corridor to purchase Twinkies and milk from a vending machine. When I could no longer do even this, Karen smuggled me an occasional sandwich from the dining hall.

I collected class notes from friends and kept at least one textbook beside my bed at all times. It took extreme effort to even pick up the book from off the floor, but I attempted not to fall too far behind in my studies. After resting most of the day I was sometimes able to make the long jaunt to get supper. Occasionally I could then go on to the weekly debate meeting or to the library for research.

Carrying my weight on the speech and debate squad was a high priority for me. I thought it imperative that I attend the state competition, which I did. The core of our team consisted of only six people. That meant each of us had a lot of work to do to fill all the different entries so we could compete with larger schools.

Generally we were responsible for two preliminary rounds each of three to four individual events, plus finals. Then there were five preliminary rounds of debate, each lasting over an hour – plus elimination rounds if we were successful. We returned late on Saturday night, huddled together in a van with travel bags and brief cases.

At the state competition I could barely walk from one room to the next to perform my speeches. In my exhausted state I was responsible for losing debate rounds because I could no longer think clearly.

My debate partner, Russ Jackson, was very worried. He graciously suggested forfeiting or allowing a younger, more inexperienced member of the squad to fill in for me. I would not hear of it. So he carried his files and briefcase, as well as mine. And I painfully limped on to each room, too stubborn to quit.

Through all this agony my family doctor merely prescribed antibiotics over the telephone. I cannot say what would have happened had I not had a scheduled appointment shortly after the state tournament. I admitted to him that I was at the end of my rope. He asked me point-blank if I wanted to go to the hospital. "What do I know? You're the doctor. Send me if I need to go," I feebly replied. He did.

The specialist who saw me in the hospital soberly informed me that I had really needed to be there at least three weeks earlier, as my kidneys had begun to shut down. At first I wanted to be given a magic drug, whatever it took so I could get out of the hospital in time to be a contestant in the Tri-Province speech tournament the following weekend.

I was to find, however, that the lupus was already so far out of control that I not only suffered from kidney failure, but had many other complications as well. I developed bronchitis and then pneumonia in one lung. My muscles and joints became weak and stiff. The skin on the backs of my hand developed a severe rash.

Even my vocal cords worsened. I completely lost my voice and could manage nothing above a whisper for a time. This meant that whenever I pushed my call light for a nurse's assistance she had to automatically come to my room to see what I needed. I could not be heard over the intercom.

During this time my blood sugar increased to alarming levels. I was stunned when one day a nurse brought in a diabetes kit and an orange. I was to read the information in the kit and then learn how to administer shots of insulin. I would practice on the orange.

I died inside, clutching the hated orange as the nurse matter-of-factly left the room. I was angry and desperate. "Oh, God," I pleaded, "please – not this. This is one thing I can't handle. Please don't make me have to endure this, too." God heard my plea; my blood sugar level returned to normal – before I even had to practice on the orange.

Gradually I realized that my stay was to be much longer than I expected. I was placed in the intensive care unit and those days marked my darkest period ever. Only immediate family and clergy were allowed to visit – and then only for ten minutes every two hours.

Much of the time I was alone with my depression. I slept a lot. When I was awake I stared at the clock on the wall opposite my bed, waiting impatiently for my next visit. Most of the flowers and cards that had been sent were no longer close by. I was only allowed to have a single plant in the room. In my misery I would not allow any form of direct light to be turned on in my room and even insisted that the blinds be kept pulled.

I do not remember having the energy to form prayers during this time. I felt too weak to rail at God or to plead for His mercy. I just felt an incredible urge to cry, to unleash the pent-up anger and resentment I had hidden for so long. But I was timid.

I didn't want strange nurses to see me cry or to take pity on my frailty. And I hated the thought of timing my tears to the few minutes my family could be present. I still clung to my fiercely independent pride. But one evening when Mom and Dad entered the room I quietly called for Mom to come close to the bed.

"Mom," I sighed, "I just want to cry."

"Jennie, it's okay to cry," she assured me. She tried so hard to be strong for me, all the while hiding her own pain.

I gave up hope of returning to school any time soon. It was too far outside the realm of possibility to even consider. I just wanted to go home.

Maybe I should have sensed the seriousness of my situation when a priest arrived to visit instead of the nuns who usually came. He softly asked how I was doing, then took my hand and prayed with me.

I learned later that I was not expected to live. I am not sure what effect knowing that at the time would have had on my will to recover. In retrospect, I can only say that I am glad I did not know my prognosis at the time.

Later, after returning to a regular room, I came to understand perhaps a portion of the agony parents go through while watching helplessly as a child suffers. As tragic as this hospital stay was, I am told that it increased their reliance on God at a time when we all desperately needed to feel the power of His presence.

For the time being, my kidneys had almost completely shut down so I was allowed only enough liquid to swallow my daily regimen of pills. I had to drink a mixture of protein to supplement all the protein that was leaving my body due to kidney failure.

The nurses did all they could to make my stay as comfortable as possible. They "flavored" the protein mixture. One morning, thinking they were doing me a favor, they brought me cold cereal for breakfast – with coffee cream on it. I was not very polite.

"What's this?" I demanded.

"Coffee cream. I knew you could not have any liquids, and I didn't think dry cereal sounded very appetizing."

"I never eat milk on dry cereal," I barked. With that, she kindly replaced it with dry, crunchy cereal, never noting my harsh tone.

Those nurses even had the courtesy to ask if I liked a little or a lot of toothpaste on my brush. They also took great pains to make sure the water for my sponge baths stayed warm, no matter how long it took to perform the arduous task of getting me cleaned up for the day.

My kidney function continued to deteriorate until only one option remained. I was set to undergo dialysis for about a month. I did not know that I was not expected to live for that one month.

I pictured an ominous, sadistic machine, but I never had to see it. The night before I was scheduled to go on dialysis, one last attempt was made to get my kidneys to function again. It worked. The disease went back into remission. I had been spared from the brink of death by what many would call a miraculous healing. And I am certain that only through God's grace did I live.

This bout with lupus caused me to rethink my theology and philosophy of life. You see, I knew what happened to me was not a healing – it was merely a reprieve.

Instead of getting better, my condition has just gradually worsened over time. I was forced to face squarely many questions that would not have been asked in other situations. Why hadn't I been healed? Why me? Why did I have to face this type of illness, with all its uncertainties? How could I go on, knowing this illness could very well kill me?

These are the types of questions I will address throughout the remaining chapters of this book. Come with me on the journey from singing hymns in the backyard to a deeper understanding of an awesome God who allows me to sing while holding onto my chronic cross.

Chapter Two:

Where's My Miracle?

Immediately upon hearing of my disease many well-intentioned people began coming to me, assuring me that I would indeed be healed. During my hospital stay, hundreds of people I had never even met were praying for me.

After my release from the hospital – escaping death at worst and kidney dialysis at best – it appeared that I had been healed, that a miracle had taken place. Actually, I had not been given total healing. My life had been spared; that would have to be enough.

My lupus still lurked beneath the surface, poised to strike. I continued to take my medicine, and had good days and bad days. Intermittent trips to the hospital at least once a year for occasional flare-ups became a fact of life. Perhaps these "minor" hospital stays were partially in preparation for the time to come.

I had been away from the dorm for over three weeks following my major kidney problems, besides the time spent huddled in my bed, too weak to attend class. When I reappeared at school after spring break most of my instructors assumed I had simply dropped out of school. Each was extremely cooperative.

My Old Testament Prophets professor, though, refused to allow me to make up a 100-point quiz. He tolerated no excused absences, whatever the reason. Still I completed the spring semester on time, with no grade less than a B.

Relationships

Remembering my senior year at college reminds me just how prone I am to stray from God. I too easily allowed both denial and pride to play havoc with my spiritual well being. The school year presented no notable health problems. My real difficulty that year was of a romantic nature. I met "Joe" shortly after the school year began. He appeared eager to date me and I decided to give the relationship a try.

Everything went smoothly – for a while. He bought me dinner and flowers often and flooded me with attention. Perhaps subconsciously he embodied the stability I thought my life needed. We began to plan a life together, yet only a few short months later I felt my life ripping apart at the seams.

Joe was intensely jealous of my friendships with others, especially those on the speech squad. Slowly I pulled away from them – to salvage our crumbling future. I allowed him to ruin relationships I had treasured for years.

Gradually, as he became emotionally abusive, I saw that my dream world had shattered. Yet much like I denied my illness, I denied even this until the damage had been done. In righteous indignation I resigned from the forensics team. As a direct result, I missed being a part of the team winning the national championship, something I will always regret. Thank God, the friendships were later restored.

I cannot blame Joe or anyone else for the mistakes I have made. I relate these events for two reasons. Following some very rough times with my lupus, some people have had a tendency to tell me how brave and courageous I must be to have come through so much.

I am not brave. My struggles with lupus and my battle with a broken relationship merely point to my desperate dependence upon God, and for His strength to be made perfect in my incredible weakness.

Secondly, I think there is a tendency to categorize people. It is easy to say, "Oh, she is the woman with lupus," or to apply some other label. But we cannot separate one part of our lives from the rest. And we cannot expect deterioration in one aspect not to have a profound impact on all other areas.

I finished my bachelor's degree, a double major in speech and psychology, and decided to pursue a career in psychology. Due to a lack of funds I lived at home again for a time.

I began my master's degree in the fall of 1985. I worked about twenty hours a week at McDonald's and undertook a full schedule of coursework at Pittsburg State University in

Pittsburg, Kansas. Going to school involved a sixty-mile drive each way. Fortunately I was able to commute with another student much of the time.

Sick Again

Soon the lupus haunted me again. In the early months of 1986 I became sick – a gradual process that once more I tried to ignore. "Not now, not when I'm trying to complete my graduate degree. I don't have time to be sick," I told myself.

Excruciating headaches plagued me most of every day, and my eyes pounded with pain. When this happened at work I quickly asked someone to cover for me. Then I made my way to the back of the store where no one could see me. I collapsed in a chair, holding my head which was hammering so badly I could hardly stand it.

I would pop a couple of aspirin, grit my teeth and force myself to go back up front to wait on customers -- before anyone noticed that something was wrong. In the beginning I was even able to mask my pain from the guy I was dating. I could barely make it through dinner and a movie, yet I still refused to slow down.

Very soon the headaches worsened in intensity. I was forced to quit work because I was calling in sick so frequently. Still I insisted on attending my graduate classes. Often that would not have been possible if I had not had a volunteer driver.

A friend or one of my sisters would drive me one hour each way and wait patiently while I sat through my three-hour class. Over time my class attendance waned, as I seemed to sleep almost constantly. I also had no energy to do my homework.

Until my parents realized the seriousness of my situation I was chided for "sleeping my life away." But it soon became apparent that another major crisis was at hand. My head and eyes ached so badly that I could no longer tolerate any form of direct light. I lay huddled in my bed in a corner of the room. My parents set a lamp close by so I did not have to use the overhead light.

Many nights Mom and Dad just stood at the foot of my bed, looking on helplessly as I lay there holding my head and sobbing. I was literally in so much agony that I no longer cared if I did die. At least then the pain would have to subside. Something had to give.

One morning I awoke after everyone had gone to work. Only my hard-of-hearing grandmother, who was incapable of managing on her own, was home. I could not get out of bed. My mind was so clouded with pain that I couldn't think clearly.

I knew I needed something to eat so I would not have to take my morning round of pills on an empty stomach. But I also knew I was not strong enough to fix breakfast, or even pour a glass of milk.

My attention focused next on trying to reach someone by telephone to help me. I knew my friend, Virginia, was at home. I wanted her to be with me, but then I reasoned in my sluggish state: "Why should I call her? What could she do, sit around and watch me be sick?" It would only make both of us uncomfortable.

I decided my only option was to call Mom at work. Surely this would qualify as an emergency. But in my dazed condition I could no longer remember the familiar telephone number. I tried to formulate the number in my mind, to no avail. And I did not have the strength to look it up.

After what seemed like forever, Mom came home for a quick bite of lunch. She poked her head into my room, surprised to still find me in bed. "Mom, I need help," I whispered lamely.

She made arrangements to stay home the rest of the day to take care of me. After that fateful day, Mom taped a large piece of paper to the wall at the foot of my bed with her work number written on it in big, bold print.

The eye doctor I went to, in a fashion reminiscent of the doctors who had previously tried to diagnose my illness, chided me for an overactive imagination. Following a very short eye examination and some superficial questions, he insinuated that I was a hypochondriac and perhaps needed psychological assistance to deal with my "problem."

The ride home that day was a long one. "Oh God," I silently begged, "please don't let this be. I don't understand what's going on. Help me!" I was confused at first. It hit me that perhaps I really was going crazy. At the same time I knew the pain was real. The more I reflected on the doctor's findings and on his arrogant attitude, the more furious I became.

My specialist eventually admitted me into the hospital, assuming he was merely dealing with the lupus out of remission. I was treated, given my first of many doses of chemotherapy, and released. Fortunately, this did manage to put the lupus under control.

In for the Long Haul

About a week later, since I still felt weak and had shown no overall improvement, I was readmitted. This time a spinal tap was taken (which involved the removal of spinal fluid from the base of my back). After the spinal tap I had to lie flat on my back for twenty-four hours. To move around would disturb my equilibrium and make me feel even worse. Before my ordeal was over, I was to undergo two more of these taps.

The spinal tap revealed that I had contracted spinal meningitis. The lupus medication depletes the immune system so the body will not attack itself. The combination of medications I was on at the time weakened my immune system to the point where I became susceptible to the meningitis.

My sister, Karen, and some college friends had just arrived at the hospital to visit me at about the time I was diagnosed. The doctors were unsure yet whether my meningitis was contagious so I was immediately quarantined.

While the tests were being analyzed at the Kansas University Medical Center nearby to determine what specific type of meningitis I had, Karen and my friends were promptly told they had to leave. They had driven over 100 miles, only to have to turn around and head right back.

I do not remember much about those early days, as I was too sick to be very coherent. My mind was clouded intermittently with pain and with the strong medications given to provide relief. I also battled nearly out-of-control blood pressure. The pills I had been taking to keep my pressure stable had little effect. Even the nurses got worried and it took several emergency injections to bring it under control.

My old family doctor visited. "Is there anything I can do for you? You just name it," he voiced somewhat sheepishly.

"Just give me a new body," I requested flatly.

Mom took off work and drove the 100 miles to stay with me as much as she could, frequently sleeping beside my bed in a recliner that I could not use. She grabbed sleep here and there but always seemed to be there when I needed something. I am sure the nurses must have appreciated the extra hand. They tried to help by bringing her a pillow, blanket, and coffee as she kept her constant vigil.

Much later she tried to describe the toll it took on her to watch one of her children in so much pain. She felt like crying herself, but wanted to be strong for me, especially since I was too sick to realize the seriousness of my situation. Finally the head nurse directed her to the outpatient room on that floor, where she was able to snatch moments alone to pray while I slept.

Pure Agony

Several times I experienced trouble breathing and had to be put on oxygen. One particular night stands out as perhaps my most difficult. I had been placed on oxygen, which I always found very uncomfortable, and was given a shot to combat the horrendous pain in my back. Its effect was supposed to last at least four to six hours.

I did my best to settle in for a restful night. When I was asleep I did not have to confront the stark realities of the I.V. fluids pouring into my body or the oxygen tube in my nose. But a short two hours later I awoke to the most excruciating pain I had ever felt in my life. My back throbbed and no matter how I tried to situate myself in the bed, nothing helped.

I paged the nurses, who did not have orders on hand to give me another shot. With tears in my eyes from the pain, I desperately begged them to do something. They agreed to try to reach my rheumatologist at home to see if he would consent to another injection so soon.

While waiting in the wee hours of the morning I tossed laboriously from side to side, careful not to disturb the tubes. I tried to focus my mind on a prayer to inform God that I had reached my limit – that my agony was unbearable – and to plead for mercy. But by then my whole being was so consumed with the torment of my back that I could not even pray.

Eventually my doctor was reached and immediately consented to another injection. I am glad I had a rheumatologist who believed my pain was real. I was put on powerful medication to combat the meningitis that seemed to be winning the battle.

A temporary small tube was inserted into my upper right chest in the hospital room. This enabled the medication better access to the spinal cord and provided an I.V. line that was used for other fluids.

The medicine, Amphotericin B, was a potent anti-fungal medication used to treat my type of meningitis, and referred to amongst the doctors as "Amphoterrible" because of its extreme side effects. But by the time the drug got through the veins to the base of the brain and the spinal cord, it had become too diluted to be of much value.

Surgery

One day a neurosurgeon entered my room holding a petite funnel called an Omaiah Reservoir. He explained that I would have to undergo surgery. I would have a hole drilled into my skull that would allow this funnel to carry undiluted Amphotericin B straight to the base of the brain and the spinal cord.

In the course of the same surgery a more permanent tube, called a Groshong Catheter, could be placed into a large vessel near my heart. The external portion of the flexible, clear plastic tube would be used for I.V. fluids and to draw blood – without repeated pokes into my already bruised veins.

The Groshong Catheter would replace the temporary tube in my chest. Both devices would give my doctor the opportunity to wage a full-scale war on the meningitis.

The day for surgery arrived. My parents and several other relatives were there. I did not know they had been told the day before by the anesthesiologist, "We can't promise you anything tomorrow."

In my groggy state, I clung desperately to the only thing within my immediate grasp. It happened to be a small stuffed animal, a lion that my sister, Susan, had loaned me for courage. I insisted on taking it with me.

Kindly the nurses let me hold on to it all the way to the pre-op room. It was pretty silly, in retrospect. But to a mind bogged down with pain and drugs, sometimes inanimate objects hold a special significance. At least it couldn't hurt me.

I am told the first thing I did upon my return from the recovery room was to call two very good friends in Texas, Billy and Becky Randles. Billy answered the phone.

"I just got my head operated on," I announced.

"Why don't you rest for now and call us back later," he suggested.

I do not remember the conversation at all, but it is something we laugh about now. I made a lot of calls to friends during my stay. I felt guilty using my parents' calling card but Dad felt it was very important. He called it "phone therapy."

The doctors later told me that I held a sort of in-house record. Meningitis is measured in terms of titers. At one point my titer ratio was one to 50,000. The only people in the hospital with higher titers were AIDS patients.

One afternoon when I pulled myself out of bed to go to the restroom, I suddenly saw two tables in front of me, though I knew there was only one. From then on I saw two of everything. Only by keeping one eye closed could I hope to avoid ambling into things.

Mom bought me an eye patch, which I traded off wearing over each eye. My eyesight did not return to normal until October, after the meningitis medication had been discontinued. My right eye was permanently weakened but it sure was good to see only one of everything again.

"Home" Health

After a seeming eternity the meningitis abated, and in June I returned home. But then the hospital came to me. Twice a week home health nurses invaded my home to draw blood for samples demonstrating my progress, and to deliver the Amphotericin B, which only stayed good for a few days at a time.

Every two weeks during that summer I had an appointment with my Infectious Disease doctor, who took a sample of spinal fluid from my Omaiah Reservoir and then gave me a shot of Amphotericin B immediately afterwards. The same procedures had been conducted in the hospital, but not right together. The first time both techniques were done with no time lapse in between, my head began to throb with indescribable pain.

We had gone to McDonald's for a quick lunch before seeing my rheumatologist. I was unable to keep my lunch down and began hyperventilating. I was rushed back to the medical building and allowed to lie on one of my rheumatologist's examining tables.

I could not be still, as the pain was simply intolerable. I became hysterical. My mother looked on helplessly as I writhed in agony, yelling, "I don't want to die! Help me; help me, please!" I was terrified and angry. Hadn't I been through enough?

31

My rheumatologist entered the small examining room with a shot to calm me down. "No, don't touch me! It's going to hurt. Get away from me!" I cried deliriously.

He remained calm. "Have I ever hurt you before?"

"Yes, plenty of times!" I shouted accusingly. I finally relented. Within minutes I felt drowsy and offered little resistance to being re-admitted to the hospital to find out what the problem was.

The general consensus was that performing both procedures so closely together created a sort of vacuum in my head, causing me to get violently ill. So approximately every two weeks during the summer when this was done, I got sick and had to go back into the hospital for several days to allow my doctors to stabilize me.

My Miracle – A Reprieve

Again the Lord had spared me. I had a new lease on life. But the questions of a miracle in the ultimate sense still bothered me. Where was my miracle? Throughout my life I had heard stories of people being raised from the dead, leprosy cured, all sorts of diseases – as bad or worse than mine – cured, by divine fiat.

Many of my visitors assured me that the same thing would happen to me. And yet there I was for the second time on the brink of death, saved again for a time but knowing my disease remained.

When I was released from the hospital the doctors told me I was not well. I had merely staved off another crisis. The truth settled in that the rest of my life could very well be a series of crises. I hoped my disease would stay in remission, but I could never be quite sure.

At my worst times, the uncertainty led me to severe depression. At my best times it led me to ask some serious questions. Why didn't I get a miracle? Certainly there were enough people praying for me. Surely if I lacked faith, there were others who had it.

I gave resolute thought, then, to the issue of divine healing, and the many flawed notions I had previously heard and believed. I realized that the world was far more complicated than I had ever realized.

Chapter Three:

The Hydraulic View of Healing

As a child I was always enthralled when it was my turn to go with Mom to the local service station while our car got repaired. I would stare in utter fascination as the car was driven onto a special lift and elevated to a height where the workmen could access the engine.

I later learned that the lifts were operated by hydraulics, or fluid pressure. Whenever the pressure of the fluid entered the elevator, the automobile on it rose into the air automatically.

Unfortunately, many people carry the theory of hydraulics into their philosophies on healing, assuming miracles will be routine. I have seen preachers on television tell crowds of swooning followers that all we need is faith and all our ills will be spontaneously healed.

The more greedy individuals assure us that giving money to them will do the trick. The process reminds me of a machine. All we do is flip on the switch and we get healing. Faith is the power for the machine and as long as we have it we are healed – no questions asked.

Tragically, this view leads to a number of practical and Biblical complications. First, if healing is automatic, why doesn't it occur in every case? Those who believe in universal healing would say, "Somewhere, faith is missing."

In other words, if someone with the alleged gift of healing, or someone who merely believes in divine healing in every case, encounters a situation in which healing does not occur, they must blame someone. Obviously, it is not their God. And it cannot be them, loaded with faith as they are.

It must be the victim. According to this equation, healing requires faith in God by the person praying, and a sufficient amount of faith by those prayed for.

A Promise of Healing

Following my bout with meningitis I was invited to attend a newly forming local Bible study in the home of an acquaintance. One of the women there firmly believed that healing in every case was certain, and assured me of my own imminent deliverance.

When I told her I had already resigned myself to the fact that God had chosen not to heal me she was literally appalled. She promptly started extrapolating scripture in a desperate attempt to prove her point. All I needed was faith in the Lord, she insisted, and I was home free.

I am convinced that the view this woman held can make it too easy to blame the victim of any suffering. I appreciated that she was making a concerted effort, based upon her beliefs, to instill hope. But it is a small step from alleging that someone does not have enough faith to asserting that they just do not deserve healing in the first place.

The practical result from this notion is that we need not be troubled by anyone who suffers and dies because, simply, they have failed. By blaming them we insulate ourselves and alleviate the need for caring. Of course, we would not make the same mistake.

The woman at the Bible study basically avoided me after that night. We had no major confrontation. We still both attended the Bible study and exchanged pleasantries but she distanced herself from me otherwise. I did not fit the mold of Christianity she had been taught.

Regrettably, when many of us encounter situations or events that are outside our scope of understanding we tend to dismiss them. To question them might upset our spiritual equilibrium. It makes me wonder where our faith really is.

Christ's Healings

Throughout the New Testament Christ actually chooses to heal people with little or no reference to their faith at all. Sometimes He uses phrases such as, "Your faith has made you well," found in Matthew 9:22. Yet in many other instances, Christ restores people with no mention of faith.

John 4:46-54 tells the story of a nobleman whose son is deathly ill. Jesus knows the man will not believe He is the

Savior without seeing a miracle. Christ straightforwardly tells him to go on home, that his son is healed.

However it is not until after the boy's father verifies that the fever left his young son at the exact time Jesus had talked with him that he believes. His faith comes after the healing, and there is no obvious evidence of the victim's faith whatsoever.

In another situation, as Jesus travels to Jerusalem along the border between Samaria and Galilee, He encounters ten men who have leprosy. They cry out for His pity. Full of compassion, Jesus instructs them to go and present themselves to the priests, a requirement that anyone healed of leprosy must complete before reentering the community.

As they go on their way they are all cleansed of their sores. One of the men returns to thank Jesus and to acknowledge His Lordship. Only after the man returns with jubilant thanksgiving does Christ say to him, as recorded in Luke 17:19: "Arise, go your way. Your faith has made you well." In this case only a single man expresses faith, and then solely as a result of the healing, not a prerequisite. Yet all were healed.

Other difficulties for the premise of automatic faith-induced healings are the recoveries of the demon-possessed. Certainly they have no control over their minds. How could they have faith? Yet Christ heals them.

In Matthew 8, Jesus orders the demons from two possessed men into a large herd of swine. After the swine then rush down a steep embankment into a lake and die, the townspeople plead with Christ to go away and leave them alone. This is a situation in which the individual is totally unaware of what is happening.

In another case Jesus heals an epileptic who is in the midst of a seizure. Clearly this sufferer has no idea what is going on at the moment.

Other examples abound. In Luke 7, Christ heals a centurion's servant without ever seeing the man. In Acts 3, God allows Peter to heal a man who has been lame for years by merely yanking him to his feet. The situation is really almost comical since the man is healed before he even knows what is going on.

Jesus also raises the dead on more than one occasion. John 11 relates the resurrection of Lazarus. No one around him believes he will be raised from the dead.

Everyone in that passage speaks abstractly of a day of resurrection or future events but no one demonstrates the slightest faith that this resurrection could occur in their midst. Mary, Lazarus' sister and a good friend of Jesus, even tells Him, in John 11:32, "Lord, if You had been here, my brother would not have died."

There is considerable protest when Jesus orders the stone removed from the front of Lazarus' grave. This time it is Martha, another sister, who voices her concern. "Lord, by this time there is a stench, for he has been dead four days." (John 11:39c) Still the people comply with their Lord and Lazarus is brought back to life.

Higher Purposes for Healing

The power of healing is not dependent upon any of us working up enough faith to automatically set the wheels in motion. It takes far more than a simplistic machine into which we inject faith and miracles emerge. Somehow there are higher purposes and determinations made.

Believers in automatic healing assume it is the right outcome in any situation, but healing may not always be the best option. Of course, this is a very difficult position to articulate unless you yourself are the victim.

In other words, it is all right for me to come to the painful conclusion that God has chosen not to heal me. But I do not believe others should impose their arbitrary judgments onto those suffering. The decisions are made at a divine level and we cannot pretend to second-guess God.

After my bout with meningitis I know I was extremely uncomfortable when a woman bluntly informed me that she had prayed for me to die. She had assessed that it was God's will. She just "knew" I would die anyhow, and considered her prayer a way to lessen the pain my family would feel by my prolonged suffering.

The Old Testament tells us that when King Hezekiah became deathly ill he begged for healing. God heard his impassioned prayer and responded by extending Hezekiah's life for fifteen years. During that time Hezekiah exposed all the wealth of the kingdom to the Babylonians, causing him to be severely admonished by God through the prophet Isaiah.

Second Kings 20:18 says, "And they shall take away some of your sons who will descend from you, whom you will beget; and they shall be eunuchs in the palace of the king of Babylon." As was predicted, Manasseh, Hezekiah's son, inherited the throne, becoming the most evil king in Judah's history. He was born during the last fifteen years of Hezekiah's life.

Until we are forced to look death squarely in the face its reality remains clouded. If universal healing did occur, there would be no death. Or if there is death, there would not be an arbitrary shortening of the life span. Even the patriarchs and saints suffered both.

Healing can only be assumed to be the best outcome in a situation if there is nothing more terrible than physical illness. The rhetoric of those who hold this view seems to belie a terror of physical suffering that borders on the pathological. There are so many worse things than physical illness.

In all of this, the nature of God is lost. He is the part left out of the equation. He is viewed as automatic, like a black box. We pour faith into the box and healing comes down an assembly line. But we are not dealing with a machine.

We are dealing with the ultimate Personality, the ultimate in Thought, Purpose, Direction. In our imperfections we can catch only glimpses of God's perfect will. The problem is not His unwillingness to share it with us, but our inability to grasp it.

The Purpose of Prayer

If in fact miracles can and do occur without evidence of faith, we are then left with two important questions. What is the purpose of prayer? And for what can we legitimately pray and expect positive results?

In his New Testament letter to them, James rebukes a group of Christians by informing them that the reason their prayers are not answered is because their motives are purely selfish. James 4:3 says, "You ask and do not receive, because you ask amiss, that you may spend it on your pleasures."
I know in my own life I must constantly question my motives in prayer. There are times I have literally pleaded with God, "Oh Lord, think how much more I would be able to do for You if I were healthy! If You only let me be free of this I could accomplish so much more."

For a long time I thought this prayer was indeed selfless. After all, I just wanted to please Him. I finally had to realize that the more selfless prayer would be patterned after Jesus' prayer in Gethsemane, found in Matthew 26:39c: "Nevertheless, not as I will, but as You will." I had assumed that God's will must include my healing only because I wanted it so very badly.

Many of us err in our prayers because we do not first seek to know the will of God. Maybe we are afraid to know. We profess that God knows best and that His ways are above reproach, yet we dread the knowing or being told no.

Seeking and acknowledging God's plan carries with it an awesome responsibility. It means we must make a decision regarding it, perhaps a commitment. It sometimes means accepting a different reality.

I know a man whose whole prayer life centered on thanking God for His goodness and asking for favors. When I questioned him about this I was told, "I don't want to ask Him what He wants from me. I'm afraid of what the answer will be."

God does not command us to pursue His will without providing the means. James 1:5 promises us, "If any of you lacks wisdom, let him ask of God, who gives to all liberally and without reproach, and it will be given to him."

Thankfully, there are several areas in which we can pray dauntlessly. Because Jesus now serves as our great High Priest, Hebrews 4:16 encourages us, "Let us therefore come boldly to the throne of grace, that we may obtain mercy and find grace to help in time of need."

Paul prayed with boldness for the Colossian Christians he had never met, asking God to fill them with the knowledge of God's will and spiritual wisdom and understanding. We can always pray that God will make us more Christ-like and know that is truly His desire.

Second Peter 3:9 reminds us that God wants everyone to come to repentance. I believe, then, that we can pray with confidence for the convicting power of the Holy Spirit to move in the lives of unsaved people and to accomplish all commands specifically outlined in His Word. Some of my most precious answers to prayer have involved claiming the promises that His Spirit will move in the lives of those who need to find Christ as Savior and Lord.

True prayer, then, as God intends it, depends upon first trusting that He knows best. It happens when what I want becomes what God wants – no matter what that entails. Faith in itself is good, but the problem of the hydraulic view of healing is that we tend to forget where we place our faith. We must put our faith in the Healer, not in the healing. The difference is amazing.

Having faith in God may not be satisfying to those who insist that their way is best and who demand immediate gratification. It is comforting to think healing can come automatically so long as enough people work themselves into the proper spiritual frenzy. It is a bit less satisfying to realize that sometimes, for no apparent reason, healing will be denied.

But in another way, it is imminently more fulfilling to know that our faith is in the Living God, not in a machine – that the source of our faith is neither hydraulic automation nor an arbitrary tyrant. There is a purpose to all we face and all we endure.

After all, which is the truer faith? A faith that rests on the promise that any time things get tough you will be bailed out, or a faith so firm it can carry you through the tougher times?

Chapter Four:

Onward from Bethesda

We all know people in our communities and neighborhoods, perhaps in our own homes, who feel that Christianity cannot function when times get tough. Karl Marx took it a step further, insisting that religion was an opiate for the people.

The hard truth is, no one is immune from suffering. Quite plainly, people die – bad people, good people, even Christians with more faith than many of us will ever rally. Tragedies such as famines, earthquakes, hurricanes and tornadoes occur on a large scale.

The reality of an afflicted world often leaves the unbelieving with the conviction that, as Christians, we are merely sticking our heads in the sand. We are ignoring a world of pain and problems, acting as if they do not exist.

I was uncomfortable with both extremes. I certainly could not dismiss my own chronic illness. I also knew that no amount of faith would heal me. A philosophy professor once attempted to clarify the phenomenon. His theory was that when sin entered the world, the concept of natural consequence did, as well.

In practical terms this meant that if I walked out in front of an oncoming car, no matter how good a person I may be, I am going to get hit. At times God chooses to intervene, and that constitutes the miraculous. The same principle is true when the crust of the earth shifts, causing an earthquake. The natural consequence is that those nearby are affected.

I returned to my search of the scriptures. I was already familiar with the passage in which Jesus assures the multitudes in Matthew 5:45b that God, "makes His sun rise on the evil and on the good, and sends rain on the just and on the unjust." I was aware that good and bad things happen to "good" and "bad" people. Further digging led me back to a Bible story with which I was acquainted but had never really examined in depth – the account of the Pool of Bethesda in John 5.

Healing at Bethesda

> *"After this there was a feast of the Jews, and Jesus went up to Jerusalem. Now there is in Jerusalem by the Sheep Gate a pool, which is called in Hebrew, Bethesda, having five porches. In these lay a great multitude of sick people, blind, lame, paralyzed, waiting for the moving of the water. For an angel went down at a certain time into the pool and stirred up the water; then whoever stepped in first, after the stirring of the water, was made well of*

whatever disease he had. Now a certain man was there who had an infirmity thirty-eight years. When Jesus saw him lying there, and knew that he already had been in that condition a long time, He said to him, 'Do you want to be made well?' The sick man answered Him, 'Sir, I have no man to put me into the pool when the water is stirred up; but while I am coming, another steps down before me.' Jesus said to him, 'Rise, take up your bed and walk.' And immediately the man was made well, took up his bed, and walked," (John 5:1-9a).

In this story, dozens, perhaps hundreds of people are lying around a pool. Jesus intentionally approaches only one man, probably stepping over the bodies of several others. He compassionately gazes down at him, and asks him if he wants to be healed.

Maybe asking the invalid if he wants to be healed seems a foolish question. But anyone who has suffered with a serious illness for any length of time will realize that it is not so foolish. In this man's case, his livelihood was most likely that of a beggar. He necessarily lived off the charity of others. His illness, in a very real sense, was also his sustenance.

I remember talking with a girl I once knew who had a very crippling disease. She told me, "Jennie, I think God is really ready to heal me but I'm not ready to be healed yet." At the time I found that statement exceedingly bizarre. Later I realized exactly what she meant.

So Christ first asks this man if he wants to be healed. The question is reminiscent of a scene in a movie by the British comedy troupe, Monty Python, called, *The Life of Brian.* In the story, a leper is complaining that he was healed without a warning. The leper goes on to explain that once he was a leper with a trade and now he is unemployed.

I am by no means trying to insinuate that most people who are sick enjoy their illness. But I do find it interesting that Christ first asks this man if he wants to be healed. The man's response is that he has no one to put him in the pool when the water is stirred.

This reply refers to the traditional story that when an angel moves the waters, whoever is first into the pool is healed. This man is guilty of the same point of view discussed earlier, that of automatic healing. If he could just get into the water all his problems would be over.

Christ proceeds to heal the man, who then saunters away with his mat. But what really seized my attention about this passage is that Christ did not heal anyone else. There could easily have been others in far worse condition than this man. Yet Christ healed only him.
In my mind, I could almost hear the cries of the others left there. "Lord, You healed him. Please, heal me, too." "Jesus, over here! My daughter is so young and helpless. Don't leave us here like this!" "I saw You cause that man to walk again. Can't You do the same for me?" "Please, let me have my sight, so I can see You, Lord."

My heart broke as I thought of Christ and how He must have felt. He knew it was not His Father's will that all those people be healed on this side of heaven. He also knew that none of them would understand.

No Apparent Pattern to Healing

The question of "Why?" kept hammering at my mind. I desperately wanted to be able to understand why the others were not healed, why I was not healed. Was this the only man with enough faith? Actually, this man did not even know who Christ was until much later. Was he the only one who deserved healing? No. In a very real sense, none of us have the "right" to demand healing.

As I thumbed through the Bible to explore other examples of Jesus' healings, I found no particular pattern. There was no special design to who was healed and who was not. Indeed, many of those at the pool may have had a firm faith in God, but for some reason they were not healed. Christ addresses the question of healing briefly in Luke 4:24-27:

> Then He said, "Assuredly, I say to you, no prophet is accepted in his own country. But I tell you truly, many widows were in Israel in the days of Elijah, when the heaven was shut up three years and six months, and there was a great famine throughout all the land; but to none of them was Elijah sent except to Zarephath, in the region of Sidon, to a woman who was a widow. And many lepers were in Israel in the time of Elisha the prophet, and none of them was cleansed except Naaman the Syrian."

Jesus tells us there were many suffering from leprosy. But only one was cured. There were multitudes starving yet only one was saved. He never says that these individuals were uniquely qualified for their deliverance. He does not blame the victim, nor praise the delivered. There is no discussion of any systematic reason why His prophet was sent, not to his home country to facilitate a miracle, but to a foreign land.

Moving On

Further consideration of the story of the Pool of Bethesda led me to realize the futility of all those who insisted on merely staying by the Pool. Life was passing them by. Instead of living with their handicaps, they were waiting for perhaps the rest of their lives for healing that may never come.

I had to recognize that I could not tarry there. If Christ wanted to heal me, He did not need me waiting by the Pool for Him to accomplish the task. It's a matter of attitude and choices. I can languish in misery, bitter because of my lot in life and always longing for something more. Or I can go on, living in spite of the reality of a chronic illness and its limitations.

In previous work with sexually abused adolescents I emphasized that they had no reason to feel guilty about what happened to them; they were not to blame. I also attempted to teach them to view themselves as survivors, not victims. The difference in outlook is essential.

A verse that has become my mantra since my lupus diagnosis is Galatians 2:20: "I have been crucified with Christ; it is no longer I who live, but Christ lives in me; and the life which I now live in the flesh I live by faith in the Son of God, who loved me and gave Himself for me."

All of us face crises at one time or another. Just because I was not chosen to be divinely healed did not mean I was to sit idly by, excused from taking up my cross of service as a Christian. I merely had a different one to bear.

I am still fascinated at the Acts 5 account of the apostles rejoicing for being counted worthy of suffering for the name of Jesus. And then I want to cower in shame at the many times I have yearned to just give up.

The story of the Pool of Bethesda does lead to a conclusion that, while not comforting on the surface, I find deeply reassuring. God does not always answer our prayers in the way we might expect. Any notions of a Jesus we can set on the dashboard of our cars or carry around in our pockets, a God we can use by manufacturing faith - these are useless.

The pagans had automatic views of their gods. With this sacrifice or that ritual, they hoped their god would perform a given action. By chanting this mystic incantation, the gods or spirits would be forced to yield to their wills.

But believers have something immeasurably more encouraging – a God of purpose and direction. I find that far more consoling than I would if I had an utterly impulsive God who was susceptible to my whims, so long as I could build a sufficient faith. It is inspiring to know there is Someone watching over me who possesses infinitely more wisdom than I have.

I have heard wonderful stories and seen people who have been miraculously healed of their diseases. And I am truly thankful for that. Just because God has not ordained my healing does not mean I am commissioned to stay and rest by the Pool.

My purpose is to go on living each day to its fullest. Learning from the Pool of Bethesda means living in spite of and in some ways, because of, a problem that does not disappear, but that our gracious Lord holds our hands through.

Chapter Five:

Denial

One of the most difficult things I ever had to do was help tell a fifteen-year-old boy that his mother had just committed suicide. The youth was in a residential treatment facility for emotionally disturbed adolescents and had long been a victim of physical abuse by his alcoholic father.

There were initial sobs of shock and disbelief. But what followed was a blatant attempt to block out the reality of the incident, a total avoidance of the situation. His unacceptable behavior increased markedly as the anger and confusion were kept bottled up inside. The staff and other male residents were encouraged to give him both time and space, but everyone was on edge as the circumstances continued to worsen.

Finally, I received a telephone call at home late one night. Would I please hurry over to the unit? The young man was sobbing uncontrollably and vomiting profusely. I shook myself awake and tore past speed limits in an effort to get there as quickly as I could.

At last the grief-stricken teenager was ready to lay aside the denial of his mother's death. There were so many issues to be dealt with that he had been avoiding by refusing to accept reality. Now he was ready to talk.

He could begin to communicate his guilt over not being able to prevent the suicide and his anger that it was his mother who had died rather than his abusive, alcoholic father.

Psychologists generally agree that the first stage for people going through a crisis is denial. Just like the boy initially blocked out his mother's suicide because it was too painful to deal with, so others in crisis situations tend to disbelieve the truth.

Overview of the Grieving Process

Psychologist Elisabeth Kubler-Ross is perhaps best known for her writings on the stages of the grieving process of the terminally ill, as chronicled in her book, *On Death and Dying.* These phases consist of five parts: denial, anger, bargaining, depression and then acceptance.

The grieving process has since been generalized to include responses to any number of disturbing realities. These tragedies may include divorce, separation, loss of a job, death of a family member as described above, or in my case, the diagnosis of a chronic disease.

Denial can probably best be defined as the refusal to accept an unpleasant reality – the "It can't happen to me!" syndrome I spoke of in the first chapter. Denial does sometimes serve a useful purpose but often it is destructive because as long as it persists, a person can never get past that point.

Often the next stage is a deep-seated anger at being forced to deal with the truth. Since it is difficult to locate an exact object with which to be angry, as in the case of an illness, frustration is frequently vented toward others who try to help us.

It may also be directed at God, whom we blame for allowing it to happen in the first place. For me, bolts of anger flashed as I inwardly shouted at God, "Why? Why me? Why now?"

For many, the third part of the grieving process involves bargaining. After the initial anger has been unleashed, the individual may feel that he has a better chance of getting what he wants by being nice. This is usually accomplished by trying to strike bargains with God.

"I'll go to church regularly," or "I'll live my life for You," are only two examples of the endless array of promises one makes on the condition that God grant them their request.

For quite a long time I refused to acknowledge that I was subject to this phase of the process. I already wanted to live my life for God. Why would I possibly need or want to bargain with Him?

It is true that I viewed my lupus as an interruption, a nuisance keeping me from the tasks at hand. But for me, the bargaining merely took on a different form.

The extent to which I would go to bargain with my Lord did not really surface until I was told of the healing of a saintly woman in the church my husband and I were attending at the time. She had been battling cancer for several years yet remained a true inspiration for all those around her. She had always been confident -- she shared with me that God was in control of her situation, no matter what happened.

My husband, Mike, and I were on our way to one of my chemotherapy treatments when I shared the unexpected good news of her healing with him. We were both very glad for her. Gradually the talking subsided and I gazed out the window. But I did not really see anything as we drove.

Tears filled my eyes and my own heart ached. "Oh, God, I'm ready. Heal me. Just think how much more I could do for You if I were healthy! And I'm young. Please heal me, too," I silently pleaded. For me, bargaining with God took the form of telling Him how much more I could accomplish for His kingdom – if only I were healthy.

The depression that follows the bargaining stage rolls in like a flood when the individual realizes that striking a deal just will not work. Finally, the acceptance comes. Only then can there be peace.

I believe the stages are basically the same for the terminally ill and the chronically ill person. The painful difference is that the chronically ill are susceptible to repeated bouts of the grieving process. These can potentially occur each time the disease fluctuates between remission and exacerbation.

With my background in psychology, I was familiar with the five stages of the grieving process when I was diagnosed with lupus. In spite of this I could not avoid undergoing those stages myself. From the initial soreness and fatigue I felt during my sophomore year of school, through each step of illness, and especially during those times I knew deep down that I was beginning to come out of remission, I tried to deny my illness.

Acting Out My Denial

Denial is an interesting phenomenon because in one sense the more emphatically we deny, the more deeply we know it is true. Oddly enough, in my own mind it was permissible for me to deny my own illness but it was not okay for the doctors I consulted to do the same.

The disclaimer may take any number of forms: refusing to go to a doctor or hospital; not taking prescribed medication or staying on a special diet; not making or updating a will; or, insisting that God has already healed you.

There were times for me when I put off going to a doctor. There are still occasions when strictly following my doctor's orders seems to reinforce the truth of my illness at a time when I feel a need to withdraw to denial again.

56

During my junior year of college right after my lupus had been diagnosed, I did everything I could to keep a low profile. I tried to hide the fact that I was on special medication. I would excuse myself to go take my afternoon naps, which had become necessities. I desperately tried to keep up with everyone else.

Each time I went to a speech and debate tournament I would challenge Ward, a dear friend of mine, to a foot race. Ward is a tall, lanky, athletic fellow, and even in the best of health I could not outrun him. But I always insisted on challenging him to a foot race. It became a joke.

"Jennie, you want to race me again?"

"You know I do. But I get a little bit of a head start."

"You're over halfway to the finish line! All right, go ahead. Ready . . . GO!"

Off we went. I always cheated. And I always lost. While we pretended it was a joke, I think everyone knew I was denying my illness. I tried to act like everything was all right, like I could keep up with Ward and my other friends.

Denial can certainly be a useful coping mechanism at times and is not uncommon among patients. There were circumstances in which I effectively used denial to ease the pain, as with the racing. At other times, I denied too much and at the wrong times.

Consequences of Denial

Through my illness it seems as if things have often gone a little too far. In retrospect, I know my denial has played a part in it. I could have learned as much as eight weeks earlier that I had a rare form of spinal meningitis had I not persisted in camouflaging my symptoms for the sake of continuing graduate school and maintaining an active social life.

Only when the headaches from the persistent fever became unbearable did my stubbornness melt. Shortly after that I wound up in the hospital.

Besides prolonging dealing with the inevitable, denial also serves as an excuse to keep others at a distance. This was especially true in my prayer life. When I succumbed to the initial stage of denial after my diagnosis I did not immediately pray for healing.

I didn't want to admit that anything was really wrong. "Nothing that a little time and a few pills could not take care of," I assured myself. I saw no need to bother God about it.

Perhaps subconsciously, I realized that if I were to approach God with the request for healing, there were many other feelings of anger that I would have to confront as well. For the time being, then, I considered it safer to avoid dealing with the matter at all and kept God at arm's length.

Denial also robs those around us of the opportunity to share in our suffering. When the wall of denial is erected, while others can definitely see that a problem does exist, the result is oftentimes pity.

We relegate them to watching us add layers of bricks to the barriers we refuse to allow them to penetrate. They surmise that it must be terrible because we are not willing to face it, much less allow them to see it.

I believe Romans 8:28 applies to the stages of an illness. This verse assures us that all things work together for good if we love God. The "good" from an illness may be in helping others learn through our sufferings. That does not make a person a martyr. It just makes them realistic and provides a sense of purpose to what we often view as an otherwise hopeless situation.

Denial can totally short-circuit the growth process. During the phases when I denied my illness I learned nothing. I gained nothing. And I did not allow those around me to learn. Yet the illness was a very real part of my life. So what I did, in essence, was to ignore reality.

We humans are not designed like flatworms. When we cut ourselves into halves, both sides do not grow independently. We grow as whole persons. To the extent that we refuse to recognize and deal with every aspect of our lives, we stifle the growth and maturation of all of it.

Denial is not an easy thing to work through because of the thin line between denying an illness and focusing on it. The doctors initially assured me that I was merely a hypochondriac. That bothered me because I thought I knew myself. The term hypochondriac did not fit what I perceived my personality to be.

Tearing Down the Walls

In one sense, I was relieved to learn the name of my illness. It finally grew to the point that I was no longer interested in denying the problem. I desperately wanted to know what it was; I wanted to give my tormentor a name. I yearned to be able to call it something because then I felt I could fight it.

Denying that an enemy exists does not cause him to fade away. The best option for facing a difficult situation is to grow into it, to take hold of it and to learn what we can from it. Only by facing the inevitable can good be wrought from the challenge.

When I look back and note my disclaimers, I regret the time I have spent in the pit of denial. My husband, Mike, and I now laugh about the extensive "to do" lists I used to prepare, trying to cram as much as possible into my day.

I insisted on writing an impossible number of things to do. Invariably I became distraught at the end of the day when I had only accomplished a small percentage of the things on my list.

Mike assured me that even a healthy person would be hard-pressed to get so energetic a list completed in only twenty-four hours. I still make my lists and try to set goals for each day. Only now I attempt to set objectives that are within reach and thus avoid a great deal of frustration.

To those who know someone currently going through this stage, let me caution you to never allow another to blatantly refuse adequate care in the name of denial.

You can gently insist on the proper management of the situation -- be it adherence to dietary restrictions or taking medication. Many times this is actually comforting to the sufferer.

Tearing down the walls that have been built by denial means that others can then show understanding and empathy, rather than pity for feelings and emotions they cannot comprehend. If I had admitted to my physical pain earlier I would have experienced much less trauma.

If I had confided my fears and frustrations earlier, I could have allowed others the opportunity to provide a ministry of understanding, of sharing in my agony by listening and of helping me face the reality of the hurt. Even more importantly, I could have relied on the strength of my Savior had I not allowed stubbornness to prevail.

On an emotional level, the best thing others can do is just to be there. We should simply listen, not judgmentally, not accusingly. We need to encourage others and quietly hold their hand, all the while leading them to a bigger, stronger Hand that can hold us when life seems too big or rough for us to handle.

Chapter Six:

Why?

Following a long bout with denial, anger gripped me solidly as I was forced to face limitations that affected my energy level, and ultimately my career. The foundation of my anger addressed the very basic question of "WHY?" It is a question we all ask, almost as a reflex, when something happens to us. "Why?" "Why me?" "Why this?" "Why now?"

When my disease initially struck, I was a young college student filled with energy and ambition. What I lacked at the time was a definite sense of direction. I knew in a vague sort of way that I wanted God to be glorified by my life. But inside I struggled with rudimentary questions about my major and where I would go once I graduated.

Then seemingly out of nowhere lupus invaded my territory. Sure, I had no concrete plans for the future but this certainly had no place. Suddenly my pace had drastically slowed due to my illness and nothing was ever the same. What I was unable to see at the time was that the lupus served as a powerful tool in determining my career and my ministry.

Questioning God's Purpose

I began interrogating God about His purpose in allowing this "awful thing" to happen to me. It is a question I asked bitterly at times. "Oh, God, why me? What did I do to deserve this?" For the longest time I did not seem to get an answer. "Please, listen to me, Lord! Don't leave me like this."

Almost daily in my work with physically and sexually abused adolescents, I heard the same question echoed as those teens sought desperately to find a reason for their sufferings. Inevitably these victims carry with them an inordinate amount of guilt.

They reason that somehow the abuse must have been their fault. If only they had tried to fight back; if only they had not been afraid to tell; if only, . . . and the list goes on.

A major part of the therapeutic process for this and many other traumatic events centers on the resolution of guilt. Of course these youngsters did nothing to deserve the abuse, any more than I deserved to have systemic lupus.

Just because people are suffering does not automatically mean they have done something wrong, that a sin has been committed. It's not that simple. Suffering does not intimate that there is a fault to be found, as some are quick to suggest.

In John 9 Jesus reiterated this point in the healing of a man who had been blind from birth. Jesus' disciples asked Him if the man or his parents had sinned, for him to be in this predicament. Note that they were already quite sure a sin had been committed. They only sought to know its origin.

I imagine they must have been astonished at His reply. "Jesus answered, 'Neither this man nor his parents sinned, but that the works of God should be revealed in him,'" (John 9:3).

Why Not Someone Else?

A second question that flows naturally from the "Why me?" is the "Why not someone else?" In my own case the generalization of this question narrowed quickly. I had a certain person in mind. I remember lying in the hospital bitterly contemplating the unfairness of it all.

I had singled out one specific individual to personify my "Why not someone else?" My person was someone I saw as contributing nothing to society, who had no goals or plans. In my very worst moments I thought, "Why couldn't it be him, Lord? Look at all the good I could be doing. He's of no use to anyone else."

My attitude was indeed uncharitable. But when I was in the midst of my suffering it would have done no good to tell me my question was wrong or un-Christian. I already knew that. I am thankful that when I finally confided my insensitivities to my mother she merely listened without preaching, and thus provided me the opportunity to work through those feelings.

In my search for answers I eventually came to the conclusion that the better question was actually, "Why not me?" There are millions of people in the world who will starve to death. There are people whose homes are destroyed by war or natural disasters.

Thousands were killed in the World Trade Center bombings. Millions were killed during the Nazi holocaust. Up to three million people were butchered in Cambodia by the insane Khmer Rouge.

I could have been one of those people. In other words, there is no intrinsic reason why I should avoid suffering. It is just not a good question. I do not believe the world is completely arbitrary. Job's reply to his wife when she suggests he renounce God captures the essence of this position. "Shall we indeed accept good from God, and shall we not accept adversity?" (Job 2:10b).

I spoke earlier of sin bringing about natural consequences. This concept seemed to vaguely point me in the direction I needed to go for my answers, but there had to be something more. It would not have been so difficult for me to understand my sufferings if I were being persecuted for the cause of Christ.

Hebrews 11 has always been a great inspiration for me. I marvel at the heroes of the faith, some named and countless numbers simply referred to as those of whom the world was not worthy. They were tortured, flogged, chained, imprisoned, sawed in two, killed with the sword, homeless and mistreated.

I had done nothing heroic. I had simply contracted a chronic illness. Hence, I reasoned that my suffering was of no consequence, which made me that much more frustrated. If I had to suffer, I desperately wanted it to be for something I thought noble and dramatic.

My Answer

I finally found what I was looking for in 1 Peter 1:6-7: "In this you greatly rejoice, though now for a little while, if need be, you have been grieved by various trials, that the genuineness of your faith, being much more precious than gold that perishes, though it is tested by fire, may be found to praise, honor, and glory at the revelation of Jesus Christ."

I realized that what God wanted for me more than He wanted me to be healthy, or rich, or powerful or anything else, was to have genuine faith in Him, to be reborn in the image of His Son, Jesus! Just as gold must be refined by fire, so my lupus was to serve as a series of trials designed to strengthen my trust and enrich my walk with the Master.

The late Christian philosopher, C. S. Lewis, compared it to a young man going to the dentist. He really doesn't want to go, yet a certain tooth is throbbing with pain. He finally relents, but he emphatically informs the dentist that he only wants the one tooth to be fixed.

As the dentist examines the man's mouth he finds that major work is needed. He cannot just operate on the individual tooth. His occupation as a dentist requires him to put the whole mouth in order.

So it is when we invite Christ into our lives. It does no good for us to merely request a "piece" of Him, just enough to get by. He wants to completely make us over to be like Him. He allows different methods to be used. My lupus is a part of my purification process, a part of my refining as a Christian.

We have to learn not to be so possessive of all we have, including our health. The measure of true Christianity is our willingness to lose ourselves in Him. And the things to which we cling too tightly – these are the things God asks us to relinquish. For only then can we have our hearts and hands free to cling solely to Him.

How to Help

For those who know people going through the phase of anger and questioning, there are several things that can be done to help. Above all, it is important not to be judgmental or to glibly quote scripture.

Chances are the person is familiar with the scripture and already feels guilty for questioning it. And if she is unfamiliar with it and angry with God in the first place, quoting something she may not believe in will not be productive.

A simple way to remember what you can do is to think of being a PAL – PRAY, be AVAILABLE, and LISTEN. Whether or not the person is a Christian or is even aware of it, you can pray for her. Just knowing others are praying for them can mean a great deal to people whether they profess to believe in the power of prayer or not.

A good friend of mine was having marital problems and confided her fears of a failed marriage to me. We knew each other well enough to know we were both sincere. Although she was not a Christian, when I told her I was praying for her, she slowly looked at me, tears in her eyes, and replied, "I'll take that." My offer opened the door for later being able to share my faith in Christ with her.

We must also remember the importance of being available to a person in crisis. Let them know you will be there when you are needed and then follow up on that. Consider not simply saying, "Call me if you need anything." People are hesitant to ask you to interrupt your already busy schedule.

Instead, offer something specific. Mow the grass; make a meal; keep an eye on the children; take someone to a doctor's appointment; clean the house. The possibilities are endless. Consider your abilities and their needs.

Finally, listen. The individual has at last come through the stage of denial and is ready to confront the reality of his situation. Part of that may encompass some emotions he feels guilty about. But denying those feelings does not make them go away. Let the person vent his feelings so he can go on.

In all of my struggles with the anger of my lupus, God taught me to pray. I became convicted to pray that when I earnestly yearned for a soul to be saved or for someone to come back to the Lord, I had to pray for the Lord to do "whatever it takes but only as much as it takes" for the prayer to be answered.

God is not vindictive. He doesn't thrive on our pain or anxiety. He only wants us to be like Him but we cannot do that unless we surrender all we have. That does not necessarily mean He will use it. He just wants us to be available.

The great paradox of Christianity is that we must first lose our lives in order to find them. A Christian cannot pray for wisdom or to be remade in the image of the Father without being willing to die to self. (He asks no more of us than He required of His Son.) Death to self is indeed painful, but it is necessary for life in Him. When I discovered this, the most wonderful reality of all, it took away my compulsion to ask WHY.

Chapter Seven:

Depression

I had successfully denied my illness for a time. I became bitter and angry about having to cope with my ailment, and had even attempted to bargain with God to get out of it. Following this I settled into dull despondency.

Depression is commonly defined as anger turned inward. That's how it was with me. I was too tired to fight what was happening any more, and sometimes too exhausted to care.

Depression Manifesting Itself

The sadness does not come in great waves. I have found that it appears at odd times and is not always predictable. It seems to rear its head at awkward, illogical times and for seemingly irrational reasons.

The first major depression I can recall occurred during my junior year of college when I was in the hospital with kidney failure and various other complications. Strangely enough, what triggered the despair was not the fact that I was on the verge of death, or that I was faced with kidney dialysis. These things frightened me.

What actually sparked the depression was the realization that I would be unable to attend the Tri-Province speech and debate tournament scheduled to take place the weekend following my admittance to the hospital. Certainly this was not a logical cause for depression, yet it dealt me a debilitating blow.

During that prolonged hospital stay depression settled over me like an unrelenting fog. These are the times, when neither darkness nor light is fully seen, that can be most intimidating. A great fit of despondency that lasts for one afternoon, while horrible at the time, is bearable.

But when depression settles in as habit – as something you go to sleep with and wake up to – it is petrifying. It dulls the senses. It feels like being in a pit with no energy to climb out.

Lying in the intensive care unit I felt trapped and my outward anger transformed into a weary withdrawal -- surrender to the tubes, the pills and the machines. I lay there in the darkness of the room, refusing to be comforted.

The minute hand of the clock on the opposite wall crawled in step to the downbeat of the ticking, the only noise of the room. The corridor noises of the flurry of machines, hushed tones, and occasional blue codes were distant and heartless.

Depression's Effect on Prayer

My depression had settled into a numb, gripping fear. I was frustrated because I wanted so very desperately to cry, yet I equated my emotion with self-pity. For the longest time I allowed myself no release.

Perhaps most disturbing of all was that I could no longer seem to pray. Sometimes I simply had no energy to frame complete thoughts or focus my mind to form my petition. Other times God felt so far away from that lonely, dismal room that I could not find Him.

I think the Psalmist must have understood the feeling of "lostness" I am describing when he penned, "Lord, why do You cast off my soul? Why do You hide Your face from me?" (Psalm 88:14).

Part of me knew I needed to get past this point. But the depression was so consuming and hopeless that I slid into laissez-faire indifference. At those times I secretly wished for death. It seemed the only way out.

It is difficult for those who have never experienced colossal depression to understand the enormity of the dullness and despair that one goes through during the dark times. The story of Elijah reminds me that anyone can be susceptible to bouts of depression.

Elijah was a renowned prophet of God who had even raised a widow's son from death. God had honored his prayer that there would be three years of drought in the land. Then suddenly Elijah's life was threatened, and he ran and hid.

Elijah was discouraged and frightened. After all, he had dedicated his life to preaching and upholding God's precepts. Now he was about to be killed. Elijah thought he was the only man left who trusted God.

"And he prayed that he might die, and said, 'It is enough! Now, Lord, take my life, for I am no better than my fathers!'" (1 Kings 19:4b). With God's help and assurance Elijah was eventually able to conquer his dejection and go on.

More Bouts of Depression

During the next two years, intermittent struggles with depression plagued me as my illness fluctuated in varying degrees of severity. My next major confrontation with it came during my battle with the spinal meningitis.

The despair did not begin as a fear of death. I was upset at the interruption in my plans for graduate school and for my future. I was discouraged and felt unable to communicate my depression to anyone around me.

My minister at the time, Pastor David McDowell, drove the 100 miles to visit several times. He encouraged me to try to talk into a tape recorder when no one else was around. He thought that doing so would at least help me sort through the confusion I was going through.

I was not interested in the idea at the time, nor did I feel like I had the energy to implement the plan. There have been many occasions since that I wish I had captured my depression on tape. Even my mother regrets not insisting that I go through with the idea.

There did come a time when I felt ready to communicate my thoughts on to paper. I had been in the habit of journaling, though I had obviously fallen far behind. One day I awoke with a little more energy than usual. With quite a bit of assistance I was transferred to a large recliner and wheeled over by the window on the opposite side of the room for extra light.

I ceremoniously opened my notebook to the page I had last written, foolishly thinking I would just sit quietly and all at once completely catch up and fill the empty pages. I picked up my pen and attempted to focus my eyes on the lined paper in front of me. It was all a blur. Now that I was finally prepared to write, to vent my deep frustrations, I could not see well enough to do it.

I was furious! In a fit of anger I threw the pen across the room, and stormily demanded help to be put back in bed – immediately. No one could console me. I lay in bed and sobbed uncontrollably until I drifted back to sleep in utter defeat.

One more crisis loomed before I was to begin working my way out of depression. A well-meaning nurse suggested I start a latch-hook project. I had never learned the simple maneuverings of the craft before, but my mother purchased a small latch-hook kit at once. It had many different, bright colors to make it easier to distinguish.

Once again I was temporarily uplifted at the thought of actually being strong enough to accomplish something, even if it was only a small latch-hook design. But my eyes could not focus on the tiny lines. In tears, I had the project put away as I retreated to the comfort of my bed.

I was overwhelmed with physical pain and too exhausted to question my plight. I was at an all-time low, and still God seemed to be nowhere around. I knew intellectually that He still loved me.

I had memorized promises such as Matthew 28:20b that assured me, "Lo, I am with you always, even to the end of the age." But I could no longer feel His presence at a time I thought I needed it most. I felt abandoned.

Lifting the Cloud of Depression

Oddly enough, it honestly seemed as if the days I was down the most and the very closest to giving up, I received literally handfuls of get-well cards, or letters, or a new flower arrangement or a visit.

Sometimes I got twenty cards a day. I propped myself up in bed and painstakingly labored over each one. Mom read them to me if I could not make out the particulars.

Most of the cards and letters were from my home church. Each silent reminder assured me that those caring people were praying for me, and that God was still in control. It was not until much later that I realized God's benevolence in the timing of those kindnesses.

Spiritually I was not yet at a point where I could acknowledge my anger at God and work things out with Him. But He could not restrain His compassion for His hurting child. So He stretched out His hand and communicated His love through others.

Gradually I grew stronger and began to regain more control of my body. I was sent to occupational therapy for approximately twenty minutes per day to help combat my depression. It took all the energy I could muster to sit up in a straight-backed chair for very long.

I used my time to sand pieces of wood to make a planter for my sister, Karen, who went to school in Bolivar, and had made numerous excursions to visit. It was not much – just a small, crudely-made planter. But that token gift gave me a purpose to get out of bed and something to look forward to each day.

In my work with depressed adolescents, the same theory applies. Getting them involved in volunteer work, whether it is with animals, the elderly or handicapped children, helps them feel needed. Involvement can begin to lift the veil of depression.

Eventually I was able to crawl out of the depression. I wish I could say that I had a flash of spiritual insight that threw open the windows for me and I suddenly strolled out into the sunlight of Christ, never to look back. Realistically, it was more like a tedious mountain climb.

The valley of depression is deep and hard, and in a strange way, comforting. So I slide back down. One of the frustrating things about depression is once you are there, it is much easier just to stay there than to work your way out of it.

I was always most depressed when I was weakest physically, emotionally and spiritually. When I was really weak it was difficult to change my way of thinking, to change my feelings, and to break out of the shell that depression built up around me.

I wish I could present a magic formula for warding off depression but I cannot, because I am not immune. I still feel it sometimes. It is not so deep or long as it was in the hospital when I felt completely separated from God and man. Just on this or that day when I am too tired to do something I really want to do, or I see my friends who have been able to capitalize on time that I have had to watch go by, it comes back.

I know all the logical reasons why I should not be depressed. I know how negative it can be. But depressed people are not looking for a sermonette or a comparison that shows us how much better off we are than someone else.

When I was told these things I felt as if my own emotions were being rejected. It was as if I had to deny my "right" to be depressed because someone else was theoretically suffering at a deeper level.

The key is to view depression as an aberration, as something abnormal and not a way of life. Paul admonishes us in 1 Corinthians 15 not to look upon death and suffering as those who have no hope.

I have come to the conclusion that the only remedy for depression is hope. Without that there is no source of strength to climb out of the pit of despair – none whatsoever.

How to Help

There are many ways we can help someone going through a bout of depression. I have already mentioned the immeasurable benefit I received by virtue of the visits, flowers and cards that were sent – simple reminders of God's grace, and the support of so many. Feeling useful by doing small tasks also did much to fill the void of emptiness.

Keep in mind not to overwhelm the person by suggesting she accomplish monumental feats. A depressed housewife who might feel completely crushed at the notion of cleaning the entire house might successfully respond to straightening one room.

It became increasingly important for me to do little things for others to help end my depression. It is indeed imperative for us to feel useful, no matter how minute the gesture. Even now when depression starts setting in once again, I try to force myself to perform a small act of kindness to take my mind off my self-pity.

One time that effort meant baking a late afternoon batch of chocolate chip cookies for about the only other person I knew in a new place Mike and I had recently moved. Encourage others to take these giving steps toward the healing process.

I did not want the pity of those around me, but my situation had severely damaged my self-esteem. Boosting the self-image of those suffering can indeed be a miracle in itself. Karen's graduation took place during my 1986 hospital stay with meningitis. The family had also been waiting to celebrate Susan's Birthday until I could be there with them.

The day for the graduation arrived. My sister, Ruth, lived near Kansas City, Missouri, where I was hospitalized. She volunteered to forego attending the ceremonies and told me she had a surprise for me. She arrived in my room and immediately went to work.

She carefully painted my fingernails and fixed my hair the best she could – considering my conspicuous bald spot left after surgery. Then she gingerly helped me into my best nightgown and waited with me until the rest of the family came.

Since I could not go to them, my family came to me. They brought all the birthday and graduation gifts, and two cakes to celebrate. The understanding nurses allowed all of them to crowd into my room.

I am quite sure that I looked very haggard lying there. I even fell asleep in spite of all the noise and excitement around me. But I drifted off feeling a bit more like a woman again. Small kindnesses mean so much.

God communicated the power of His love and the hope that I so desperately needed through the little things so many people have done throughout my illness. I have learned that, although Christ is not really the bridge over troubled waters, He never stops leading me through them. And that is what enables me to continue.

Chapter Eight:

Loneliness

Whenever I go through a bout of depression, I find that loneliness is never far away. Loneliness is sort of the little sister of depression. Before I continue, let me clarify that being alone and being lonely are two entirely different things.

It is natural to want, even need, to be alone at times. I am talking here about the aloneness that accompanies depression, occurring just as easily in crowded rooms as it can in the quiet confines of a hospital bed.

This is the aloneness that cries out for someone to simply be attentive to the needs of the sufferer. Loneliness and depression can interact, each one contributing to the other. I was always depressed when I was the loneliest. And my depression always made me lonely because I felt no one could really understand what I was going through.

I sensed distance from the world around me. Loneliness hemmed me in with constant grogginess, the endless routines of hospital life, pain and even the tiresome whirring noise of the humidifier.

Human beings, no matter how much one may wish to deny the need for it, are intrinsically social animals. God created us to thrive in the company and support of others. After He put the first man on the earth, God recognized his need to experience companionship. "And the Lord God said, 'It is not good that man should be alone; I will make him a helper comparable to him,'" (Genesis 2:18).

Sociologists now know that small babies must be touched and held in order to thrive. Part of the growth and development of normal children involves the establishment of friendships with peers. We learn early to share confidences of joy and pain, and the importance of listening to others. In doing this we cultivate meaningful relationships.

Loneliness assumes a life of its own when you are on the verge of dying. I felt so utterly isolated and abandoned when my parents hesitantly sat down by my hospital bed during my first lengthy hospitalization and told me that in the midst of my worst times in I.C.U. I had not been expected to live.

I know they would have gladly offered to go through any necessary pain to relieve my own agony. But I felt that death was something I had to face alone. That emotion triggered my loneliness. My isolations did not stem from a fear of death, but from the secret dread of facing it by myself.

How could I even begin to approach God with this problem? (It is odd how we Christians hold "secret" thoughts, thinking we will simply not pray about them, thus keeping them from our Lord.) I was ashamed of the way I felt.

I knew in my heart that I was a Christian. I knew that dying meant going to heaven with all of its bliss. But my humanity made me afraid to go through it by myself. And I was worried that God would not understand my timidity.

Jesus' Loneliness

I am reminded that Jesus is both fully God and fully man. I imagine that while Jesus was on earth, He never felt loneliness so desperately as when He agonized in the Garden of Gethsemane.

He had taken His disciples there to wait with Him before His arrest. He had even taken the three He was closest to, Peter, James and John, farther into the garden, and requested them to pray for Him.

The disciples fell asleep and Jesus spent that last bit of time alone. God discerned His turmoil and sent an angel to strengthen Him for what was to come. However, it was even following that point that Jesus' struggle climaxed.

"And He was withdrawn from them about a stone's throw, and He knelt down and prayed, saying, 'Father, if it is Your will, remove this cup from Me; nevertheless not My will but Yours, be done.' Then an angel appeared to Him from heaven, strengthening Him. And being in agony, He prayed more earnestly. And His sweat became like great drops of blood falling down to the ground," (Luke 22:41-44).

I am amazed when I contemplate the love God showed us when Jesus came to the earth and really experienced all the trials and temptations we go through. He understood my loneliness. That meant I did not have to be apprehensive about admitting my fears to Him.

In fact it is precisely because He allowed Himself to face the same vulnerabilities that He can now be our Intercessor, or High Priest, with God the Father. "For we do not have a High Priest who cannot sympathize with our weaknesses, but was in all points tempted as we are, yet without sin. Let us therefore come boldly to the throne of grace, that we may obtain mercy and find grace to help in time of need," (Hebrews 4:15-16).

The thought was indeed liberating. How I wish I had realized it at the time. The knowledge would have saved me much unnecessary self-seclusion.

As it was, I had an unhealthy preoccupation with death for a period of time following my release from the hospital. I often lay awake at night worried that I would die in my sleep. I became petrified at the notion of ever having to return to the hospital. I was actually less afraid that I would die, than that I would die without being aware that I was dying.

I have discovered that when I am lonely I am invariably consumed with thoughts of self. I cannot be concerned about others because I am living in a bubble, filled with considerations of my worsening condition, or wary at the idea of death. What deepens the isolation is the feeling that those around me will not understand or will attempt to provide a pat answer to immediately eliminate all my worries.

Lloyd John Ogilvie, in his book, *The Beauty of Sharing*, describes self-concern as a dull, dark dungeon. Mr. Ogilvie posits that we must go to God to get rid of the imprisonment. I knew that was true. I needed to approach God.

But how could I do that, full of fear and anxiety as I was? Didn't He expect more from me? I still believe the ideal is that we first move toward God. But I also think that sometimes, when we feel unable or unworthy to go to Him, He sends others to us to bridge the gap.

Ministering Through People

During a particularly dark time in the hospital one of my good college friends, Nancy, came to visit me. My face was swollen because of the tremendous dosages of medication I was taking and my head was partially shaved after the meningitis surgery. I was in severe pain, and she found me deeply depressed and indescribably lonely.

Nancy immediately recognized that I was not up to a rousing conversation. Most of the time she was there, I just cried. She did not say anything to me. She did not try to convince me that my lot in life was good or that I had it "much better than so-and-so."

She merely sat and held my hand, and watched me cry. Then as the sobbing finally showed signs of subsiding, she drew close to me, and held me in her arms until I pulled away.

I will never forget that almost completely silent visit. For that day, Nancy was the strength I did not have. God had used Nancy's arms to hug me. And it felt so good.

Depression is terrifying. But depression coupled with loneliness is virtually impossible to overcome. Without loneliness to feed it, depression is much easier to leave behind. That day a part of my loneliness left me.

On a more humorous note, I remember my sister, Karen, trying so hard to keep me in touch with my friends and family while I was hospitalized. She often drove nearly 100 miles from college in Bolivar to visit, bringing several friends with her.

One night they traveled all that way and even smuggled in a pizza after hours so we could have a party. Unfortunately I must have been given a sleeping pill and fell asleep shortly after their arrival. I fought the drowsiness, but I just could not stay awake.

Even though I did not get to fully experience the pleasure of their company, I deeply appreciated their coming. I know their class schedules were demanding, and that driving all that way was a real sacrifice. I will never forget their thoughtfulness because it helped to break that pattern of loneliness for me.

Oddly enough, there were times in my loneliness when I wanted to pretend everything was all right. I longed to convince myself that I actually preferred being alone, and lonely.

I daresay all of us are guilty of masking our true feelings of need and of pushing others away when we do not wish to confront the problem, or are afraid the other person is not genuinely interested.

My advice to anyone who is with someone suffering, whether from the loss of a loved one, an illness, a divorce or any other type of personal crisis, is not to believe the outward signs that indicate they want to be completely alone. Sometimes they may so forcefully insist upon being alone that their wishes must be honored. But do not assume they want to be alone, even if they imply that.

Sometimes the best therapy, indeed the only therapy, is having a companion. I am grateful that those who know me best did not rely on the verbal and nonverbal cues I periodically gave about wanting to be alone. Instead they came and joined me, and helped me work out of my depression and loneliness.

Many people are uncomfortable being with those who are sick or in mourning. Prior to entering the hospital with kidney failure I dated a guy I will call Bob. He was so distressed at my illness that he failed to contact me in any way while I was away from college, not even upon hearing that I was in intensive care. Each day I waited expectantly for a card, flowers, a phone call – anything – to let me know he was concerned.

Nothing came. I was hurt, and his lack of contact led to the collapse of our relationship. Our dating came to a formal end shortly after my return to school. What I want him to know is that I understand his timidity. No one is expected to be comfortable in those situations or to automatically have the right words to say.

Those of us who have gone through hard times know there are no magic answers and we resent being told that there are. Just having someone to come and care, to hold one's hand, is enough to help. The best comfort of a suffering person is to have someone be there for a little while.

God sometimes uses hard times and trials to make us more like Him. One of my most difficult tests has been loneliness in the midst of depression. But beating the dread of loneliness is not so hard. All it requires are some kind words and a good friend to hold your hand. That's all the magic there is to it.

Chapter Nine:

Shattered Plans

Most of us truly believe we are going to be around five years, ten years, perhaps even twenty years down the road. Therefore we naturally tend to set goals and make long-range plans. Our lives are so ordered in this day and age that we have to do this.

It would be foolish for a twenty-year-old not to begin plans for his future financial security. It would be unwise for a thirty-year-old not to prepare for his children's college education. The making of plans – even long range – is a necessity.

What I quickly found when my illness came upon me was that I could no longer make firm plans. On the most immediate level, it once meant the inconvenient interruption in my plans to attend a major speech tournament. I felt strongly that I had let everyone down by not attending. Throughout the rest of my college career, my illness and other relational conflicts disrupted and minimized my speech and debate career before I ever really accomplished all the goals I had set for myself.

Although it seems like a small thing now, I remember once wanting to do extremely well in a particular debate round. In all honesty, it was a measure of revenge. My partner and I were scheduled to debate against a guy I had formerly dated.

"Rob" had dated other girls without my knowledge while we were going out – in spite of a mutual agreement that neither of us would. Now was my chance to really show him up.

I entered the round, fully prepared to launch a harsh attack on the case Rob and his partner presented. But despite my strongest intentions I just could not stay awake. I kept dozing off in the middle of my opponents' speeches, and even my partners'.

I was unaware, disconnected from what was going on around me, and completely unable to concentrate. My partner understood, and did not get angry when we lost that round.

After that trying round, my debate coach insisted that I cut down on the number of individual events I performed at each tournament so I would still have some energy left when it came time to debate. I loathed having to "ration" my energy. But that was now the only way I could stay awake. As it was, I was known to sometimes grab a quick nap before a round – if I could find a sympathetic teammate close by who could be on hand to wake me up in time.

Even if unimportant in the entire scheme of things, we all cling to certain small areas of our lives for assurance, confidence, enjoyment and achievement. Speech competition was one of mine, and I was intensely disappointed when my lupus forced me to slow down. I knew then that many of the goals I had wanted to attain in this area of my life would never be realized.

Becoming Disheartened

When I graduated from Southwest Baptist University in 1985 I lived at home for a time. I solidly determined not to allow a broken relationship or an illness keep me from getting on with my life. I had wanted to enroll in a top graduate school to pursue my psychology career.

I dreamed of obtaining my doctorate and becoming a big name in the field. Instead I found myself juggling a job at McDonald's and driving back and forth to school in the evenings from my parents' house.

As is so typical of us when we get frustrated, I became disheartened with God. After all, I felt I had been led to strive for a career in psychology. I needed at least a master's degree to do that. And I could go so much farther with it if I went to a bigger school with more notoriety! Didn't He know that?

"Lord, You must have put me here for a reason," I finally acknowledged. "I definitely had other plans in mind. Help me accept whatever it is You have in store for me."

Even as I uttered this prayer, I dismally felt I had settled for less than what I might have achieved under different circumstances. One thing I am still struggling with is not to second-guess God, for there are times even now when I wistfully think of what I may have done. Those are the times I am in the midst of self-pity and selfishly wish God would go back in time and undo so much of what has happened.

No Children of My Own

I couldn't see it then, but God was indeed shaping my future through the haze of my shattered plans. For one thing, I was living at home when I contracted spinal meningitis. Yes, I became quite a burden both physically and financially, on my parents. But the situation I was in meant my family was right there when I needed them most.

Of much greater personal significance, though, was a discovery in May 1986, immediately before my long hospital stay with spinal meningitis. In order to effectively deal with the out-of-control lupus, my rheumatologist was forced to change my regimen of medications to include a type that was considered experimental for lupus patients.

He stood quietly against the wall near my hospital bed, unable to look directly at me, and informed me that I needed a form of chemotherapy called Cytoxan. It was to be administered every two to three months, depending upon my condition – for an indefinite amount of time.

He went on to say that before I signed the release form for this treatment, I should know there would be a forty-five percent chance of sterility. Then almost as an afterthought he added, "But you can't get pregnant anyway." He later made clear that, although deciding to get pregnant would ultimately be my decision, in all likelihood I could never carry a "fetus" full term.

That simple statement shattered me. I have always loved children and looked forward to the time when I would have my own family. Even if I had never wanted to have children, just knowing that it was no longer feasible made me feel somewhat helpless.

It is difficult to express the agony. It seemed I had lost my sense of womanhood, my sense of worth, and in the end, my sense of purpose. Of all the results of my illness, this was the most devastating.

It has taken years for me to allow God to melt away the bitterness and resentment within me. Indeed the struggle with this loss was much more difficult when I saw so many cases of child abuse and neglect paraded before me at work. And for a long time I had to fight back tears when a friend would excitedly show me the nursery she had set up in eager anticipation of her coming newborn.

God's outstretched arms of love never stopped holding me all the times I cried out to Him about the gross unfairness of it all. And His divine mercy was magnified beyond measure as He shared our grief after a failed adoption.

When waves of intense emotion settled over me, I eventually learned to cling fast to the knowledge that God is still in control. He is still on His throne. And best of all, He is never surprised by anything that happens.

Graduate Work

Another area of my plans that has been directly affected by my illness involved my graduate work. I had resolved to complete my graduate degree by July 1986 so I could get a job and finally be out on my own. When I became sick and even after I entered the hospital with meningitis, I emphatically informed my parents, "I intend to keep this deadline! I can still do it."

They did their best to reassure me that my graduate work was not the most important consideration at that point. But I refused to listen. Graduation for me meant independence and freedom. I would not let go of that dream and all I could think of for the first few days in the hospital was how far behind I would be when I got out and how I would be able to catch up.

As my condition continued to deteriorate I made a concession that I would perhaps put graduation off until August, giving me one extra month to finish my practicum. That was my final offer. Under no circumstances would I put it off any longer.

In spite of my best-laid plans, I became sicker than anyone realized I would. Soon I forgot all about my schooling for the time being and concentrated on only one thing – staying alive.

What that incident of stubbornness showed me was how utterly fantastic our priorities can sometimes become, and how any illness or other catastrophe can totally change what we regard as most important in our lives.

My highest priority when I went into the hospital was merely finishing school. Then it slipped to going back to school. Finally my intention was just to be able to go back home.

Eventually I did finish my M.S. in December of 1986. That delay reinforced for me that we do not have complete control over our own timetables. We live in an era of deadlines and commitments. But these all-powerful deadlines are simply specter rising up in our lives, seemingly full of substance. In reality they are merely shades with no meaning.

Following my release from the hospital I relied on my family for literally everything – shelter, food, medication, helping me hook up to my home I.V.s, transportation and even reading my assignments to me when my eyes hurt. Due to the severity of my shattered plans my self-esteem had suffered a tremendous blow.

Where was my life to go from here? I felt as if I was stuck in the town I had grown up in, living with my parents with no way out.

God's Patterns

Looking back, I see a definite pattern of planning God was using that affected several major areas of my life. I was asked to lead a girls' teen mission group at church. The nucleus of about five girls slowly blossomed. I later made the group co-ed and experienced great success.

Gradually the church began to refer to me as the youth director. All my work was voluntary, but to me it was a calling. I loved those kids, some of them enthusiastic Bible intellectuals who had grown up in a church setting, others from broken homes who felt trapped, some who had never heard the gospel story.

I went into the homes of the youth, and did my best to live the faith I so strongly professed. I felt useful again. God directed the time I had so desperately fought for as my own to introduce me to a need I might otherwise have never seen.

Had I moved from Nevada when I had planned to, chances are slim that I would ever have met my husband, Mike. At the time he lived about sixty miles away. We were introduced through his cousins, who were my old speech colleagues. I am still amazed at how God conquered my pride after my break-up with Joe to restore friendships with people who would ultimately introduce me to my husband.

My illness, though shattering my plans at the moment, helped shape my entire future. I do not believe God causes tragedy to make things happen. But I am convinced that He can use even the most devastating event to His glory.

Even knowing all this, I still have a tendency to try to take on too much. Part of it is probably denial rearing its ugly head. Part of it is the piece of me that insists on making plans and saying, "This is what I'm going to do, okay, God?" and not waiting for an answer.

When I was finally able to work again I experienced great difficulty staying awake. In the middle of the afternoon I found myself fighting off sleep in the confines of my office, sometimes unsuccessfully. I always completed my work on time, and I was very conscientious about doing it well. But the lupus made me tired, and there seemed to be nothing I could do about it.

Facing Reality – with God

I have gradually come to understand that part-time work is much more realistic for me. No, it is not what I originally planned at all. I will never be a big name in my profession. But now that I am not seeking the notoriety of fame, I can concentrate more fully on what should have been my priority all along – making others familiar with the name of Jesus Christ.

During those times when I get discouraged about my lack of ability to do all the things I plan, I try to remind myself that Paul, the greatest missionary of all time, made tents for a living. His primary goal was to share the good news of Christ with others. His work was merely a means of financial support for him. Through tear-stained eyes, I bow my head and whisper, "God, I am willing to 'make tents' – if it would bring glory to Your name."

Many of the deadlines we set are completely arbitrary, designed to give our lives meaning. We puff them up as important but they too, eventually fade. We need to realize that our lives are more important than these artificial barriers. We need to transcend the manufactured limits we place on ourselves.

Indeed my illness has taught me that long-range plans are tenuous things. None of us really knows whether we can fulfill those well-laid ideas. Auto accidents, fires, illnesses, a death in the family, any one of thousands of things can interfere and shatter those plans.

We must attempt to exploit the day, the moments we do have. We need to make those long-range plans in the sense of giving our lives order, purpose and direction, but only for that.

The key to life is in the living, day in and day out. That's become acutely significant to me now that I grasp how suddenly my health can take a downhill turn. It could very well lead to another hospitalization, incapacitation or even worse. In one sense it is a haunting feeling. Yet it forces me to make a choice involving what is truly important to me.

Will I allow the conflicts and fears of a foreboding and uncertain future to rob me of the enjoyment of the present? It is a fundamental question we all face, directly or indirectly.

Each of us will face shattered plans, some worse than others, but surely we will all face them. We must examine our lives and our priorities, and submit them to God. It has been my experience that His ways are best.

If you know people who are suffering in the midst of their shattered plans, do not simply rush in and tell them that, "It must be God's will." Do not conduct a behind-the-scenes investigation into whether sin led to the catastrophe. This is not our place.

Just be there to help them pick up the pieces. If and when they are ready to talk about it, then you can show them how God can work through any situation. I am grateful that God is not limited to only what plans my finite mind can conceive.

The question is, "What happens to our lives when our plans are destroyed?" Will we treat them as they truly are — artificial, the means to an end? Or will we let them control our lives? We must never allow our plans to become the tail that wags the dog.

Chapter Ten:

Stoicism

Almost immediately upon hearing that I had lupus, I decided I would be strong. I would be a brave martyr with my condition as my cross or my thorn in the flesh. I do not know what it is about our society that on the one hand teaches us emotions are acceptable but then tells us we must bear our sufferings quietly, solemnly and with dignity. Time and again we receive the implicit message to hide our emotions beneath a mask of self-confidence and assurance.

Stoicism, the ability to face head-on what must be done without complaint, is indeed necessary at times when there is no room for fearful emotionalism. It does have several useful functions.

We cannot spend our entire lives with our emotions on our sleeves. To do so means everyone knows our most intimate thoughts, which makes us extremely vulnerable. People who bare their Achilles' heel to the world strike us as odd and difficult to be around.

Useful Stoicism

Stoicism can also serve to complement bravery and provide encouragement to others. In the World War II Battle of the Bulge the Germans had Bastogne surrounded. Yet when they demanded that General McAullife surrender, he sent a one-word written reply: "Nuts!" His stoicism among his men helped strengthen them and enabled them to continue in battle until General Patton arrived with reinforcements. Bastogne was not lost.

Perhaps the greatest account of stoicism in the Bible is found in the account of Noah. Because of the tremendous wickedness of man, God decided to send a flood over the entire earth, destroying nearly everything He had made. He shared His plans of annihilation with the one man who had stayed faithful in spite of those around him.

God instructed Noah to build an ark, a huge vessel designed to hold and protect Noah and his family, as well as large numbers of animals. Up until the time of the flood, man had never seen rain. God furnished necessary moisture by providing dew.

Noah and his three sons spent years building the ark, amidst the scoffing and jeers of many who looked on in contempt. I can just imagine them yelling, "Look, Noah, you've been working on that big ship for years now. Give it up! You say there's going to be water coming out of the sky. Where is it? When is it coming?"

But Noah believed God and continued steadfastly in his assigned task. When the rains finally did start, God closed the door of the ark behind Noah, his family and all the appointed animals. Only they were saved.

Indeed all of us, to a degree, have to maintain a sense of decorum and restraint from other people. If General McAullife had bowed to the pressures around him or if Noah had succumbed to the mocking of the mob, neither would have seen the accomplishment of his labor. The true usefulness of stoicism is that sometimes we maintain distance to keep our diligence; sometimes we cope inwardly with problems we face.

Maladaptive Stoicism

Beyond this limited function, however, stoicism can be a maladaptive, harmful pattern of behavior. At first my stoicism was partly an extension of denial and of an exaggerated need for dignity. An invisible force coerced me to sleep when I wanted to work, haunted my joints, played havoc with my education and career, and caused all manner of bizarre and unusual physical reactions to take place inside of me.

I resolved to regain control of my life, to put the best face on it. For me, this involved a great deal of internalization. If I did not parade my fears and sensitivities to others, I reasoned, then eventually I would master them.

Unfortunately I attempted to extend this masquerade into my relationship with God by distancing myself from Him. My attitude became one of, "Look what trusting You got me! I'll take it from here." It hurt too much to admit I needed Him then more than ever before.

I knew deep down I would have to undergo trials and testing to become like Him. It was all well and good to pray that He would make me the kind of person that would bring Him glory and honor.

Now that my prayer was being answered it turned out to be not at all what I had expected. At the time I just wanted out. For me, being stoic meant hiding behind a facade of not needing help from anyone.

Much later I was told that my rheumatologist did not know how to cope with what I considered the proper way to handle this difficult situation. He remembered my initial reaction when he first broke the news to me of my diagnosis. He said I just lay there in my hospital bed and did not utter a word.

There were no questions, no remorse, no indignation, any of which he would have expected as a normal response. He left the room to hold a quick conference with my nurse in the hall. He wanted to know if perhaps I was "slow" and had not understood what he said.

I also carried my stoic method of coping into other areas of my life. At one point I was taking as many as twenty-seven pills a day. Yet there were times when I sought to mask my condition, even in the hospital.

I refused pain pills or other medication to help me sleep. Only pure physical torture forced me to quickly give up that area of stoicism. But it was still difficult to allow myself to unwind.

I really enjoyed relaxing in the hospital's private bath after I got strong enough to get in and out with assistance. But I was 100 miles away from my home town so most of the people who visited drove a considerable distance. Many times I relinquished the opportunity to soak in the warm bath. I should not be bathing if someone were to come to see me.

Once I insisted on walking down the hallway with my sister, Ruth, to reach the outside lobby on my floor. I knew I was not strong enough for such an undertaking even though it was only a few yards.

I really did not think anything would happen in such a short time. However, I could not make it the full distance without getting violently sick – much less make it back to bed without help.

I was excited when a nurse asked one day if I would like to join her for lunch in the cafeteria. I slowly donned my robe and we walked gingerly down the hall toward the elevator. It took all the energy I could muster just to carry my tray to the table and hold my head up to eat.

My nurse knew I was exhausted. I was grateful when at last we were headed down the hall to my room. I was anxious to crawl back into bed.

But when I turned the corner there sat three of my good friends from Nevada. They had patiently waited for me to return and were definitely in the mood to talk. I later learned that despite my feeble attempts to stay awake, my nurse finally requested that they leave.

My friends had been in my room for over an hour but I was not about to let them see my fatigue. I stubbornly viewed it as pure rudeness, never stopping to think that they did not come expecting to see me be the picture of health or energy.

To some extent our strength may encourage others but we often fail to realize how much damage it does. Perhaps the most poignant example for me occurred during my senior year in high school. Amidst my closest friends at the time there was considerable turmoil with intra-family strife.

I resolved to be a pillar of strength for them, a shoulder to lean on. It worked for a while, until one day the massiveness of the situation caused me to break down.

I entered my first hour band class with a red, swollen face. It was obvious I had been crying. My good friend, Beth, glanced at me and whispered, "I always see you smiling, no matter what. It sure is good for me to know you can cry, too." Oh, to what great lengths we go to appear controlled.

Before I began writing this book I surveyed the thoughts and perceptions of those who had been involved in my care. In doing so I learned for the first time that the nurse who had managed my case over the summer when I returned home had found me cool and distant and hard to get to know.

Eventually we became friends, but for a time my exaggerated need for strength created walls I simply would not allow people to penetrate. They made me into a cool, aloof person that I did not want to be, and sometimes became without realizing it.

Just beneath the calm surface of stoicism were actually storms of confusion and trouble. I was filled with resentment and bitterness. But I did my best to hide them, to not even admit they existed. It did not occur to me that those closest to me already saw my hurt. By refusing to deal with the reality of my illness I was also not allowing them to help me through this struggle.

I have since come to realize that the expression of emotion in crisis is okay; it is healthy and normal. It's all right to be scared and cry. And if we are resentful or bitter it does no good to pretend we are not.

We cannot hide our thoughts from God and He does not expect us to do so. We can talk to Him, even about our doubts and confusion. We must acknowledge what we feel before we can work through it.

We have to understand our emotions before we can put them into perspective. These sentiments can usually be shared with one or two people who are closest to us, who unconditionally accept us as we are.

Facing Challenges

For those who are selected as confidants, it is good to remember that while the physical pain may be difficult to cope with at times, it is the emotional stress, the underlying agony of the soul, that is probably the hardest to deal with day in and day out. All these negative feelings, the conflicting tides of passion, threaten to completely overwhelm.

Reading through the book of Job, I was impressed by the strength of his personality. I don't think his character developed only because he held so tightly to his faith in the midst of extremely trying circumstances. It was because in doing so, he allowed himself to be human, and to honestly express himself to God.

In Job 7, verses 11 and 16 we find: "Therefore I will not restrain my mouth; I will speak in the anguish of my spirit; I will complain in the bitterness of my soul. I loathe my life; I would not live forever. Let me alone, for my days are but a breath."

Job would not be moved from his trust in God, yet his human nature cried out in pain and confusion. And God did not turn His back on him when Job was harshly honest in the expression of his emotions.

When dealing with people in crisis it is difficult to know what lies beneath the surface of the stoicism. As I previously mentioned, for me it was a stuffed lion named Courage that helped enable me to let down my guard on my way into surgery, when I was perhaps the most frightened of all.

In many cases we do not know what might melt someone else's wall. We may be unaware of what can touch them deeply and provide that anchor to reality they so desperately need. A touch, a visit, a card, a flower, a balloon, or a little stuffed animal may mean more than you know.

Often it may not really matter what the particular item or action is; it really is the thought behind it. I suppose if I had picked up the lion in the gift shop myself it would not have held much meaning. But it personified for me a wide range of affections, prayers and support from my family and friends.

On a lighter note, one particular occasion comes to mind in which my stoicism abated for a short time and I was able to laugh and enjoy life. My sister, Karen, and a couple of friends had come to the hospital to cheer me up. I was in an especially good frame of mind already, and I felt stronger than usual.

An old custom of ours when entering any hospital had been to see if we could sneak into the maternity ward to look at all the newborn babies. Someone suggested that with me already a patient, this would be a prime opportunity to try it again.

Before I knew it there was a get-well balloon someone had graciously brought stuffed up one of my oversized hospital gowns to make me appear pregnant. My robe was draped loosely over my enlarged body, and I was helped into a wheelchair. We set out, first checking to see that the nurses' station we had to pass was temporarily vacated.

We did make it to the maternity ward – where I was stopped and questioned by a nurse. I didn't get into any real trouble but we were sternly ordered to return to our own floor. We hastily retreated amid healthy peals of laughter.

I have learned that part of allowing ourselves to be human is to be able to laugh. That little excursion to a forbidden area of the hospital, although not orthodox or proper, helped eliminate a small part of my stoicism.

Unfortunately, when there is a wall around someone, you may not get to appreciate the value of what you do for her immediately. You must be content doing what you can. Let God work the miracle.

When someone persists in being resolutely stoic, continue to quietly offer her a hand of support. In a nonjudgmental way, let her know you accept whatever emotions she displays. Psychologist Carl Rogers referred to this as unconditional positive regard.

The key is in listening, and in performing little kindnesses that most likely will not be forgotten and can make a real difference. I believe this is what our Lord had in mind when He exhorted us in Galatians 6:2, "Bear one another's burdens, and so fulfill the law of Christ."

Chapter Eleven:

Humiliation or Humility?

Our struggles manifest themselves in a variety of ways. But in the end we all have similar choices about the way we respond to suffering. One of the most difficult conflicts in attempting to maintain a person's sense of self throughout a crisis or an illness such as mine is that battle between humiliation and humility.

An individual needs to feel intuitively that he is somehow productive and useful. Instead, many of us succumb to the temptation to be utterly humiliated by the things that must be done to or for us. I have discovered that it is sometimes difficult to preserve an unpretentious attitude when the façade of independence is gone and the sense of shame and degradation creeps in.

My own battle with dignity began with small things. I found that I could not squeeze my own toothpaste onto my brush. Later I did not have the stamina in my arms to hold up a small hair dryer long enough to blow my hair dry.

These are, of course, slight, inconsequential situations in the whole scheme of things. But I was disturbed when I was forced to look on as more and more of my autonomy was being robbed.

I had prided myself as being fiercely independent and enjoyed doing things for myself. Now gradually my life was becoming one of reliance on others. The line for me between humiliation and humility became increasingly hazy as my condition worsened.

"Oh, Lord, I feel like I'm falling into an abyss of physical helplessness, and I detest this. Please, just fix it," I pleaded. In spite of my pleas, however, my level of dependence slowly expanded.

I began having trouble just summoning the strength to get in and out of bed to travel the few feet to the restroom that was next to my bed. Mom was near much of the time and never objected to my late-night calls for assistance.

She would take hold of one of my arms as I turned my body towards her. Then I stretched out both arms and she pulled me up out of bed. I leaned on her as I made the short jaunt back and forth.

I had no idea that matters could get still bleaker. I had always thought I would never consent to toileting assistance beyond what I already required. I consoled myself with the thought that I had reached the climax of my reliance, that I had been through enough and that God would not permit anything "worse" to happen.

I found that hoping and even praying does not necessarily make things so. I continued weakening to the point that the nurses eventually had to place a portable toilet beside my bed. And finally there came a time when even the portable toilet represented too much effort and a catheter was inserted.

Oddly, the prospect of both forms of assistance was met with strong resistance. But when the time actually arrived and the need was evident, they both seemed a great blessing. I welcomed them and they made my life much more bearable at the time. Necessity does strange things to a person's sense of pride.

I was not so humble and accepting when it came to bathing. I was embarrassed not to be able to wash my own body. I had to submit to the services of a nurse cleaning me in bed like a child. I felt helpless and exposed.

Later I progressed to the point where I could sit in the hospital shower on a plastic bench. Before I stepped into the shower the nurses were always careful to wrap my Groshong catheter (the long pliable tube extending from my upper chest) in plastic coverings to keep moisture away from the actual point of entry into my skin.

Then there was the long process of redoing the I.V. hookup and redressing the Groshong. But at least I felt I had a little more dignity.

When I gained sufficient strength to pull my legs up high enough to get into the hospital bathtub, it felt good to sit and soak – alone. Thankfully there was a cord to pull when I was ready to get in or out. There was always a nurse close by to lend a much-needed hand.

When I finally returned home I was still not strong enough to stand up for even a short shower. My mother put a small wooden chair in the tub where I sat to take my shower. That old chair had been around for years and no thought was even given to the extravagance of purchasing a plastic chair.

At this time my eyes still saw double without my eye patch and in the shower my eye patch only got wet and smeared. So I tried to take a shower with one or both eyes closed much of the time. It gave me a headache to keep looking at two of everything. And reaching for two bars of soap when there was only one made things difficult.

When I completed my shower Mom or one of my sisters assisted in lifting my legs to get out. They had to dry my legs and feet as well, because I could not bend over to reach them.

It was hard to let others help me. I felt I was a burden to my family and friends and yet I knew I needed them more than at any other time in my life. No one tried to rob me of my dignity. It was something I held within myself. At times

I wanted to rebel. At times I was appalled by my dependence.

Back Home

When I returned home I found that dressing, too, became an arduous, painful experience. I began wearing clothes that were the easiest possible to get into given the condition of my joints. I wore loose-fitting clothing that didn't require a lot of effort to put on or take off. The few times I wore pullover blouses I had to ask for help to take them off. I wore no make-up for several months because it seemed extremely tiresome to apply and remove.

It is curious that, although my physical appearance reflected my overall outlook of being tired and lethargic, there were still elements where I allowed pride to leak through. I could not even be completely responsible for my own bathing and I wore unattractive clothing - yet I decided I needed my hair done right away.

Sharon Borders, a beautician from my church, graciously agreed to cut my tussled hair shortly after my return home. I was driven to her place of business and eagerly informed her that I wanted my hair done just like my sister, Susan's.

"See Susan's hair, all nice and curly and feathered so well in the front? That's how I want mine to be."

"I'll see what I can do," she softly replied.

She did the best she could, snipping away while once again I kept my eyes closed to avoid seeing double. When she finished, I glanced expectantly into the mirror she held up for me. My haircut did not look at all like Susan's. I still had the big bald spot where my head had been cut open for surgery.

That's what I had really wanted her to somehow disguise, but there was not enough hair to cover it. I had known it all along. But I was humiliated, nonetheless, having to finally admit that it would take several months for my hair to grow back. I tried to hide my disappointment. After all, my hair did look much better than the mop it had grown into in the hospital.

"But it just isn't fair, God!" I protested loudly inside myself. "Now everyone, even people I don't know, will look at me, and point and stare, wondering why my hair is partially shaved off. Can't I have any pride left at all?"

Karen and Susan were the two siblings living at home while I recovered there so they took on quite a bit of responsibility for my care, especially after Mom returned to work. At that time I was taking close to thirty pills a day. I still slept a lot since I had little energy to do much else.

Karen volunteered to keep tabs on my medication. She knew precisely what pills had to be taken when, and with what. She took on the role of nurse, counting out my pills and waking me up to take them.

I had to be plugged into my home I.V. for four hours every day. I could not see well enough to hook myself up yet and using the Groshong catheter meant that no one had to worry about finding a vein to puncture. The I.V. hooked right into the end of the catheter.

Dad knew I was unable to walk more than a few halting steps at a time. He was able to borrow a wheelchair for me to use. In the cool summer evenings my sisters and I would go out and I would allow myself to be pushed up and down various side streets.

Those wheelchair outings were tiring for me and I never lasted long enough for Susan. She was always ready to go back out again. I think for the first time I understood what it must be like for someone without the gift of effortless mobility.

When I felt well enough to resume my studies and begin making up my incomplete grades my eyes were still very weak. I could read some, but not nearly enough to finish even one reading assignment in a single subject.

Once again my sisters were close by to lend a hand. Although I am quite sure my textbooks were extremely boring to them, they took turns reading to me until I was gradually able to do more of it for myself.

Eventually I was even able to drive again, which made me feel so much better about everything. But unfortunately for me, during one of my first excursions back out on the road I drove over a curb at the edge of the church parking lot that I had been unable to see in the darkness.

I just could not seem to get the car back onto firm footing. Thankfully, several men were on hand. It took only a matter of moments to put everything in order but it did shake my confidence more than a little.

I became a financial burden, as well. It was indeed a blessing that I was able to stay on my parents' medical insurance as long as I needed it, for the cost of my treatment would have far exceeded what I could ever have hoped to pay.

My parents have spent an enormous amount of money helping me through my illness. This included meeting deductibles, purchasing medications, making innumerable trips back and forth between Nevada and Kansas City, losing time from work and countless other hidden costs.

Learning Humility

As I look back now, I do not think I think I lost my dignity by surrendering to the inevitable. I think instead, that it removed an unhealthy sense of pride. I had a choice between humiliation at having to be dependent upon the help of others and accepting that same assistance in an attitude of humility.

I am quite certain that none of the people who helped me did so maliciously or with the intent of putting me in their debt. The way I responded to the help I received came from inside of me. I had to decide whether to be humiliated or humbled, based solely upon my level of pride.

God's Word is replete with situations in which individuals are forced to choose between humiliation and humility.

Second Kings 5 tells the story of a Syrian soldier named Naaman who was struck with leprosy.

A young Jewish slave girl unselfishly suggested that he see the Israelite prophet, Elisha, who did not even go out to meet this high-ranking official. Elisha sent a servant out to his gate to inform Naaman that if he really wanted to be healed he must dip himself in the muddy Jordan River seven times. Naaman was appalled.

"But Naaman became furious, and went away and said, 'Indeed, I said to myself, "He will surely come out to me, and stand and call on the name of the Lord his God, and wave his hand over the place, and heal the leprosy." Are not the . . . rivers of Damascus better than all the waters of Israel? Could I not wash in them and be clean?' So he turned and went away in a rage," (2 Kings 5:11-12).

He was forced to choose between a damaging sense of pride and the simplicity of spirit that eventually allowed him to acquiesce to his healing. The clouded waters of the Jordan did what no other river could because God ordained it in teaching Naaman a larger lesson.

Yet Christ continues to be the ultimate example of humility. He was arrested; he was beaten; he was spat upon; He was mocked; He was even crucified. But in all of this He was not humiliated – because He chose to submit to those barbaric tortures. When He prayed, "Thy will be done," in the Garden of Gethsemane, He had already humbled Himself for the coming events.

The soldiers tried very hard to humiliate Him. But they could not because He was not brought there by force, as they arrogantly assumed. He came to that point in His life willingly. He made a gift of His life. It is not something anyone took from Him.

Becoming a Christian involves humility. In one way it is comparable to some of the things I was faced with in my illness, although on a different plane. I had to decide whether I would accept the help others lovingly offered at a time when I really had little choice at all. I needed their assistance just to survive.

A person without Christ has to decide whether or not he will humble himself to accept the gift of eternal life. The real difference is that in the latter decision, the stakes are much, much higher.

Few of us would say we are unwilling to help others. But being unwilling to allow others to assist us is arrogant. If we refuse to let others help us it seems to imply that we are better than those we help. How can we claim to rely on Christ and to really trust in Him, if we are not willing to let those around us help?

I have never seen Christ. He has never picked me up and placed me in a wheelchair. How can I claim to trust Him to bear my burdens if I do not trust the people I can see who have helped me?

I am reminded of the story of the sheep and goats in Matthew 25. The Lord commended His followers for feeding Him when He was hungry, giving Him a drink when He was thirsty, taking Him in when He was a stranger, clothing Him, looking after Him when He was sick and visiting Him in prison.

The people wanted to know when they had done all those things. Jesus replied, "Assuredly, I say to you, inasmuch as you did it to one of the least of these My brethren, you did it for Me," (Matthew 25:40b). They were helping Christ by helping others. In the same fashion, I am trusting Christ when I depend upon His people.

Benjamin Franklin once said that if you really want a man to like you, get him to do you a favor and he will be your friend for life. Frequently we make our best friends when we reach out to someone when we are weak and show them an exposed side of ourselves. We give them the honor of assisting us through the struggle. Often we never love someone so much as when we have picked him up and helped him in his time of need.

The question then, is whether one chooses to respond to dependence upon others with humiliation or humility. Where is that line between dignity and pride? When do we, in the name of self-respect, actually engage in activities that cost us more than they are worth?

Chapter Twelve:

Dying Grace

Launched in 1977, the Voyager I and Voyager 2 robot spacecrafts are responsible for much of what we now know about the different worlds in our solar system. Both Voyagers explored Jupiter and Saturn but only Voyager 2 went on to visit Uranus and Neptune. It was known from the beginning that neither spacecraft would ever be able to return to the earth but instead be forced to wander aimlessly in space.

NASA invited a group of individuals to design messages to be affixed to the sides of both spacecrafts, intended for any intelligent life forms that might one day be exploring their worlds and stumble across them. Included was an interesting mix of communication.

Each Voyager left with a golden phonograph record encased in a golden, mirrored jacket. Among other things, this contained greetings in fifty-five human languages and one whale language, a sound essay that included a kiss and a baby's cry, 118 pictures on our science and civilization, and ninety minutes of the world's greatest hits. Some of what they incorporated in this section included classical and folk music, a Navajo night chant, a Peruvian wedding song, Bach, Beethoven, Mozart, Stravinsky, Louis Armstrong, and Chuck Berry singing "Johnny B. Goode."

I was singularly impressed by the list of inclusions in the messages to a potential "other world." We have no evidence of life in outer space. If there is, we obviously don't know how to communicate. So a group of people gathered to comprise their best attempt to understand what might be out there.

Imagining Heaven

I believe we approach death in much the same fashion as the Voyagers approached space. As Christians we have the hope of heaven but we don't have a lot of concrete information that tells us what heaven will be like.

It is difficult to imagine anything outside of what we have experienced or have knowledge. We can't build a technologically advanced machine to fly around heaven, take pictures and analyze it; and the unknown is intimidating.

When confronted with my impending mortality I was forced to deal with a philosophy that has grown popular in religious circles in recent years – the doctrine of dying grace. The essence of the principle is that when we face the specter of death, God will grant us some additional measure of strength or will to get us through our trial. Religious philosophers call it dying grace, an extra dose of mercy from the Father when we face that final journey.

The reasons for this teaching are clear. Most of us who are honest with ourselves, Christian or not, must admit that death is a disturbing thought. Of course if our faith is strong, we have the conviction that we are heading to a new world and a new life that God's Word promises is far better than what we have here. But the word "better" is often a poor substitute for "familiar."

Sometimes it is hard to imagine a world that is completely different from that in which we live and operate on a daily basis. So we devise ideas and notions that we hope will help us make the transition. And we delude ourselves with familiar symbols to describe the unknown, to make the confrontation less overwhelming. When someone dies, for instance, it is tempting to tell others, "She is asleep," or "She has gone on a trip," rather than verbally cope with the reality of death.

Throughout the years my friends and I have offered each other a sort of standing invitation, all done in fun, to try to ease the intimidation of the prospect of death. "I just can't wait till I get to heaven. I'm going to beat you in a football game on the crystal lake. We'll get to play with Moses and

Daniel and Paul, and all the others. Whoever gets there first can go ahead and start lining up teams."

There is also talk of a long celebration. "Okay, sign up now. There's going to be a party at my mansion that I figure will last at least a thousand years. Who wants to come?"

Of course we also talk about learning to fly effortlessly among the clouds. These ideas may sound humorous, or even sacrilegious. But they are merely an attempt to place something about which we know and are familiar, into something we know little about.

Helping Us Understand Heaven

Jesus understood our trepidation of the unseen, and used parables to convey many of His teachings about the kingdom of heaven. In Matthew 13, He talked about heaven in terms of planting and sowing, a mustard seed, leaven, a hidden treasure, a pearl and a net. He used common and conventional references we could comprehend to help explain the extraordinary.

Further symbols for the other world include trees, rivers, gemstone foundations and gold. I wonder if most Christians honestly believe that heaven is going to look like an obscene expression of wealth or that the key to heaven is a river in the sense that we understand it – running right down the middle of streets of gold, and then on down past gemstone foundations.

These images may be made for the purpose of encouraging. They tell us that everything that is best, most precious and most valuable to us in this world is found in a more fulfilling way in the afterlife that the Lord has offered us.

The Greek philosopher Plato had the essence of the truth in mind when he suggested the idea that this is merely a world of shadows, of images of what real life is all about. We may firmly believe, on an intellectual level, that the next world is infinitely superior to the one we now have.

We may even somewhat understand the complexities of heaven being real, as opposed to earth's world of shadows and dreams. But it is difficult to give up our stereos, our nights on the town, tasty pizza, time with friends and good movies, for something we cannot tangibly grasp.

Though these things seem trivial, we know them and the pleasure they can give us. Perfection in its highest form is still unfamiliar to us, and may not be as comforting as my brown stuffed chair or old blue jeans.

 Death can indeed be a radical transition, something we ultimately have to face alone. I can clearly understand the reason for the teaching of dying grace. However, I can't agree with the premise. The Bible, in Hebrews 11, tells us that we are to view ourselves as pilgrims on this earth. We are strangers passing through.

We are reminded in 2 Corinthians 5:17, "Therefore, if anyone is in Christ, he is a new creation; old things have passed away; behold, all things have become new." The old sinful nature we possessed before we surrendered our lives to the Lord for salvation is already dead. That means death merely serves as a transition to the eternal life in heaven we have been promised.

Life and Death as a Dance

In *A Grief Observed*, C.S. Lewis compares the death of his wife not as an interruption of loving her, but as the next part of a continual dance. Death is an absolute certainty. The dance can't be stopped but is transcended if you will, to another dimension.

The way we resolve to confront death expresses how we have dealt with life. If we cling desperately to this life, as if that is all there is, we are going to be disappointed when death and all that follows greet us.

There are some individuals who anxiously await their own deaths, and eagerly anticipate meeting God. There have been at least two occasions in my own life that I actually preferred death to the pain of the present moment. In my case, I was simply looking for an end to the suffering and death appeared to be the only way to alleviate the agony.

It seems rather odd, but when I honestly felt I was close to death I wasn't afraid, but welcomed it. However, when I looked back later, somewhat removed from the power and intensity of the moment, I became frightened. The changes in the way I approached God at those different times reflected my variable attitude.

In the midst of severe pain, I cried out, "Oh Lord, I just don't see any other way out. I can't stand it anymore; please take me home." At other times I was more inclined to pray, "Just a little longer here, Lord. I have so much left to do. I'm not quite ready to go."

When I feel apprehensive about going somewhere I have never gone for all eternity, I am reminded of the story of a young child and his mother who are trapped in a cave.

The boy has never seen the outside world. All he knows are the gray walls and the dampness of his surroundings. His mother speaks fondly of the outside world. She tells him of grass and trees and flowers, of sunshine and beauty.

With her pencil she attempts to draw pictures of what she remembers and hopes for. But her son can only grasp the one-dimensional monochromatic scrawling of shapes he has never seen. Despite her best attempts to convince him of the great world beyond the cave he cannot envision it because even its description surpasses his imagination.

The same is true of us when it comes to heaven. Jesus tried to share with us glimpses of the glories of heaven. But we can't really imagine its entire splendor because we have not yet been shown its glory.

God means for us to enjoy life and to achieve specific goals we set for ourselves. Ironically though, life on earth can be fully satisfying only if our heart's treasure is being kept for us in our ultimate destination.

If we firmly believe that our faith rests in the Creator and Sustainer of all life and the Giver of order, then exactly to the extent we are in touch and in tune with Him, we are in touch and in tune with the natural order of life. Part of that order is the transition from this physical life into another form of existence. Death is natural and inevitable. How we face death is directly a result of how we lived our lives.

As I looked death in the face, I never saw any evidence in my life of any extra grace. I found that I faced death with exactly the same number of weaknesses and vices that were in my life before the crises. And if I face death tomorrow, I firmly believe that I will face it with the same the amount of strength and faith I have developed today. And I will face it burdened with all the vices and weaknesses I have today.

Dying grace can be a comforting doctrine. Though the phrase never appears in the Bible I won't dogmatically insist that it doesn't exist. I have merely seen no evidence of it. I don't think we get anything special before we die. We have to build up that special something while we are living.

Chapter Thirteen:

Suffering on a Scale

One fear I have when I discuss my condition is that it will cause people to feel embarrassed by their own sufferings. In the hospital I fought for my life. But I saw others who were sure to lose that fight. Some people suffer much greater pain than I have, although at times that is difficult to imagine. Others have lost control of their minds or suffered the loss of a loved one.

I can honestly say that I realize there are people in worse conditions than I am and I'm thankful my situation isn't that bad. It's like the familiar story: I was sad because I had no shoes, until I met a man who had no feet.

We can always find someone who suffers more than we do. However, it's wrong to demean what a person is going through by suggesting that others are in more pain.

Suffering actually occurs on a scale, not only in levels of degree, but also in the type of anguish.

Measuring Pain

There are probably objective measures of pain, and some pain is more agonizing than other kinds. This is suffering of degree. There are also sufferings of kind. A person whose marriage is shattered after many years endures a different kind of pain than a person undergoing an operation. Yet both kinds are extremely real.

In my own case, when the physical pain is at its worst I can think of nothing else. My whole being is absorbed with agony. When I reach my own "ten" on the scale of suffering, God seems so far away I can no longer find Him. In the haze of pain and medication my mind can't concentrate to form a plea for help or deliverance.

It is always in retrospect that I realize God holds my hand through the roughest times. He has never failed to provide for me, often using family and friends to accomplish His purposes. At the very moments I can no longer reach out to Him, in His love He reaches out to me. What a God!

Deuteronomy 31:6 reminds me of God's promise to strengthen us: "Be strong and of good courage, do not fear nor be afraid of them; for the Lord your God, He is the One who goes with you. He will not leave you nor forsake you."

Beyond the physical pain, a much more enduring type of distress occurs with the longevity of a chronic illness. The intermittent physical suffering is actually short-lived when compared with the accompanying fears. There are apprehensions of an uncertain future, the realization of career limitations and the overwhelming feeling of letting loved ones down by being a burden, just to name a few.

In the midst of my most excruciating physical pain I feel alone and isolated. In this way, types of suffering can be very similar. It can allow us to more effectively empathize with others who may be fearful of the future, or lonely, or frustrated, for completely different reasons.

Caution against Comparisons

Both scales of suffering touch all our lives to some extent. When a person is suffering more than he has ever suffered before, it does little good to tell him, "Be grateful. There are many others in worse conditions." He can't picture anything worse than the amount of pain he is already experiencing.

I remember visiting with Billy Randles (a friend of mine from the speech squad I have mentioned previously) after my operation with the meningitis. He had also had an operation, his involving some nerve damage. After telling me about his situation, he announced, "But I'm sure that's nothing compared to what you've been through." I looked at him somberly and replied, "No, there's no way for either of us to know that."

It may well be that on an objective level Billy's amount of pain may not be equal to my most extreme anguish. But when anyone reaches that point of the most severe misery he has ever experienced, it is useless to tell him there is more out there. He can't conceptualize it because there is no comparison base.

Suffering always filters through the mind, the soul and the background of the person enduring the pain. Those standing by have no way of knowing how much a certain amount of distress affects an individual. He may be more sensitive to physical pain than emotional pain. How a person reacts to any incident is based upon the sum total of his previous experiences, as well as his perceptions of them. In that way, suffering is very personal and unique.

This doesn't mean that an individual can't be empathetic to a different kind or level of trial. What it does mean is that the real limits of his empathy can extend only to the degree of pain he has experienced. When I consider human limitations in this area, I am grateful that God has no restrictions on His ability to understand our agony.

It is precisely because each person's scale of suffering varies, and because we don't know what another individual's "ten" on the scale may consist of, that it is singularly unfair to dismiss someone's despair with statements about there always being something worse. That is a tool each of us should only use on ourselves.

Suffering indeed rests on a scale. None of us should be embarrassed when we seem to have reached our limit just because others have endured more. Maybe it can inspire us. Perhaps it can call us to something higher. But we need not be ashamed. We don't have to feel chained to the great stories of human endurance because we don't know exactly what those people were going through.

Daniel and Paul

Two Bible characters, Daniel and Paul, both suffered much in order to uphold their values and beliefs in God. In Old Testament times young Daniel, captured in a foreign land, refused to bow to idols or be unduly influenced by pagan tradition. Ultimately he was thrown into a den of lions because he insisted on maintaining his active prayer life.

Paul, the first missionary in New Testament times, was severely persecuted for preaching the gospel of Christ. He had been beaten, stoned and shipwrecked. He had been hungry and cold. Imagine Daniel and Paul in heaven, comparing their plights.

"Daniel, you cannot even begin to imagine the physical torture I went through! It was almost unbearable," asserts Paul.

"That's nothing! I was alone in a strange country. There were only a few of us who still held out for God. At least you had the support of all those churches you helped start," rebuts Daniel.

Pretty ridiculous, I think we all agree – just as ludicrous as it is for us to try to compare ourselves with each other, or with the great heroes of the Bible. There is nothing wrong with admitting weakness. If we never acknowledge being frail and spent, we would never be able to rely on the strength of Christ.

The person in pain is desperately seeking compassion. In his mind there may not be anyone in a worse situation at that precise moment. There may be no one on earth more depressed, more in agony, than the individual you are speaking with right then.

Being a PAL

Do not pity a person in pain, but do not deny his anguish. In an earlier chapter I spoke of being a PAL. Remember to Pray, be Available, and Listen. Give your friend permission to be depressed, to feel pain, rather than pretend there is nothing wrong. How tragic it is when we glibly instruct someone to simply "pray about it," and march away thinking our duty is ended.

In the dungeon of distress we do not need a recitation of scripture or a sermon. We need the love of God. And we are never so blessed as when God chooses to use us to express that compassion. We get to be the conduit of His grace – the hands and feet of Jesus.

God is not sadistic. He doesn't delight in our misery. But I have seen many times in my own life when He has used adverse circumstances to bring me closer to Him. When things are going well in my life it is so much easier for me to close God out, to forget how much I really do need Him.

Sometimes the only way He can get our attention is when we need something. I have learned to rely on Him much more in my feebleness than I ever did in my strength. All too often one is desperately ill before finally seeking the Great Physician.

Chapter Fourteen:

Sides of God

If a specific group of people were asked their favorite part of museum, there would doubtless be a variety of responses. Some would say that a certain art exhibit is by far the best attraction. Others would likely prefer a prized collection of aged books signed by their authors. Still others might insist that the re-creation of the room of a famous individual with all of the person's original furniture is the most extraordinary exhibit.

There is not one correct answer to the question of which museum display is the most magnificent. The various responses given reflect the different biases and backgrounds of the people who were polled. It is very likely that the display an individual had been exposed to and studied the most would be his favorite.

In many ways the concept of polling people regarding a museum display can be applied to the assorted manners in which we view God. It is simply impossible for us with our temporal beings, to fully comprehend the omnipotence of God. God is just too large, too complicated and too intensely real for any of us, with our finite minds and our finite senses, to be able to grasp all of Him at any particular moment.

Looking at God and expecting to see all of Him would be a little like being dropped in a wheat field in Kansas and expecting, with our naked eye, to see the entire earth.

Though the horizons might appear a long way off, we would still be unable to see the larger cities of Joplin, Wichita, Manhattan and Kansas City - let alone get a real glimpse of the Rocky Mountains, the Pacific basin, or the steppes of Russia.

Even the four men who recorded the life of Christ in what is now referred to as the Gospels in our Bible portrayed different aspects of our Lord. I am certain that what each of these men wrote is accurate and inspired by the Holy Spirit. But some were present for events that others did not see.

Those who witnessed the exact same event may have been particularly impressed by one thing and others by another. In the last Gospel, John describes the difficulty of attempting to convey Jesus' earthly ministry in a single book. "And there are also many other things that Jesus did, which if they were written one by one, I suppose that even the world itself could not contain the books that would be written," (John 21:25).

My Side of God

One of the great blessings of my illness is that it has enabled me to see a side of God I would not otherwise have seen. I see and feel a different part of God than the man healed at Bethesda because I am not directly familiar with the God of healing. I have instead witnessed a series of reprieves.

Following my bout with meningitis I attended a fellowship in the basement of my home church one evening. I was still at the point where I walked very hesitantly. I had a patch draped over one eye and the bald spot from surgery was still visible. A woman confidently approached me with the bold assurance of a tiger about to pounce.

"Honey," she crooned in her sugar-sweet voice, "I just know God will never let this happen to you again." She grabbed both my hands, as if to wring away any lingering doubts. Instantly I was forced to stifle a flash of anger.

I loathed her suave attempt to pacify me and to make blind promises that we were both fully aware no one could guarantee. I looked her straight in the eye and shot back, "Ma'am, sometimes the miracles of God are miracles of endurance, not of healing."

What the woman didn't realize (and what I could have explained in a much kinder tone), is that the side of God I have been given to see and experience is the side that lends strength through my most difficult crises. My view of God shows me Someone Who is still willing to love me, to care for me and to stand by me at my very worst. Because I haven't been allowed to see the side of God that completely heals, I see the side of God that speaks of perseverance and of overcoming in spiritual battles.

Biblical Examples

For examples of some of the many other sides of the vastness of God, we have only to skim through the Bible. Joshua, who led the Israelites into the Promised Land of Canaan after forty years in the wilderness, found the God of conquest and successfully developed battle strategies to take the land.

Jonah discovered the God of persistence. He found that God was more determined that he should preach the message of deliverance to the enemy than Jonah was to avoid it. Job learned the side of God that is patient and longsuffering.

David saw a special side of God in His divine forgiveness. King David had an affair. The woman got pregnant and David had her husband killed in battle by sending him to the front line.

He and Bathsheba paid the heavy price of the death of that child. But it was after David repented that he experienced the forgiveness of God. And God allowed a son of that union, Solomon, to become the next king of Israel.

King Solomon obtained a special look into the wisdom of God. God was pleased with Solomon's behavior at the time, and informed him that He would grant him a request. Instead of greater wealth or fame Solomon requested more sound judgment and understanding. And in the New Testament, we see the Apostle Paul, in the midst of hardships suffered while relaying the Gospel to others, learning about the God of endurance.

I mentioned that I was precluded from seeing the side of God that heals. Those I just referred to were perhaps prevented from seeing a different side of God based upon what paths their lives took and what God had planned for them. Apart from our circumstances, I believe that to a large extent we are limited to seeing varying sides of God based upon our lack of desire.

Discovering another side of God carries with it an awesome responsibility. Joshua could not have known the God of conquest without risking his life going into battle. Jonah was constrained to follow God's leadership at the price of being swallowed by a great fish beforehand. Job learned about the God of patience, but only through extensive and hurtful trials and tribulations.

King David experienced the forgiving hand of God and the consequences of sin as well. Solomon's increased wisdom carried with it the responsibilities of the kingdom and the admiration of national leaders who looked to him for guidance. And Paul could only see the God of endurance by undergoing the accompanying adversities.

It is too easy to become content with our little glimpses of God. We don't want to see too much because it might disturb our habits and ways of life. We might feel compelled to make changes. We might fear being looked upon as fanatics by the rest of the world.

In Matthew 25, Jesus relates the parable of the talents. In the story, a man preparing to go on a long journey entrusts his property to his servants. To one he gives five talents of money. To another servant he issues two talents and to a third, one talent.

When he returns, the first two have doubled their talents. The third, having hidden his in the ground, only returns the man's original investment. In his master's fury, the man is brutally punished, with this stern admonition: "Therefore take the talent from him, and give it to him who has ten talents. For to everyone who has, more will be given, and he will have abundance; but from him who does not have, even what he has will be taken away," (Matthew 25:28-29).

The third servant had no desire to enhance his position, to search for ways to please his master or to experience the joy of a job well done. As a result, he found the side of the wrath of God. Like the other two, he was given an opportunity to grow and improve. He left it untouched.

Sharing Our "Sides"

The sides of God are so diverse because He is so intensely real. Those who would slander our faith contend that it is merely our imagination, an opiate or an escape from reality.

But God appears that way only to those who haven't searched for His vast greatness or wanted to see even a glimpse of Him. He is ready and willing to show Himself to anyone who truly desires to find Him.

Jesus makes this clear in a portion of what has become known as His "Sermon on the Mount." "Ask, and it will be given to you; seek, and you will find; knock, and it will be opened to you. For everyone who asks receives, and he who seeks finds, and to him who knocks it will be opened," (Matthew 7:7-8).

When I become too content in my current perception of God, the Holy Spirit gently chides me to look a little further, to dig a little deeper and to search a little more – to grasp more of Him. That is one of the key reasons why spending time with other Christians, drawing from their strength and support, is so vital. This is especially true in hard times. Every Christian, based upon her own personal background, studies, and perceptions, has a bit, a piece, an insight that I can learn from in my meager attempts to see more of God.

The man from Bethesda whom Christ healed discovered a new and different side of God. Those of us whom Christ chooses not to heal, for whatever reason, learn about the God of mercy in a more complete way. We need to be careful, though, in our search to find other sides of God. We must be tolerant of those who see primarily a different side of God and who may come from another perspective. We can't second-guess God in what He shows of Himself to us, or to others.

My dominant view of God is as a Father. He is Someone Who smiles and holds me to His breast, and still offers to carry me even when I rail against Him or grow angry at things I can't understand. My God views me in my weakness as a small child He cherishes and cares for despite the fact that I am not always so lovable. He is a God that will cause me to endure.

I have described my side of God partially to give Him thanks for all He has done for me and partially to encourage each of you to show me your side. I need to know the sides of God others see to which I am now blind. We all need to share with each other. Only then can we gain a more complete understanding of the great omnipotence of our God.

Chapter Fifteen:

Quiet Saints

During the past couple of decades we have been inundated with widespread reports of improper behavior among so-called leaders in our churches. Indiscretions include sexual inappropriateness, tax evasion, fraud and misappropriation of funds, just to name a few. It is no small wonder that those within the church cringe as the name of the Lord becomes associated with such blatant horrors. Those outside the church point accusingly and say, "They are no better than I am. Why should I become a Christian?"

Just a cursory look at the Bible quickly shows us, however, that the problem began long before. Indeed, Jesus' era on earth was plagued with religious fanaticism that pretended to have a corner on the market of favor with God.

The Pharisees, whose name is derived from a Hebrew word meaning "separate," find their origin after the time of the prophets. In the beginning, the group was composed of godly men who sought to keep alive reverence for the law among the people.

But the movement grew until it resulted in a radical strictness that overlaid the law. Traditional interpretations were added, which these men claimed were given orally to Moses by God in an effort to explain the written laws.

Through their public display of worship these Pharisees sought to convince others that they were more spiritual, and therefore worthy of special preference with God. It was this group, the religious rulers of the times, who were actually the perpetrators of the majority of Jesus' persecution.

Jesus rebuked them in Matthew 23:3b-4: "But do not according to their works; for they say, and do not do. For they bind heavy burdens, hard to bear, and lay them on men's shoulders; but they themselves will not move them with one of their fingers."

Real Christianity

Confusion as to what a Christian really is, or should be, has been one direct result of the countless counterfeiters who have haunted us down through the ages. Many have come to wrongly view Christianity as a list of things to do and not to do. In fact, Jesus made it paradoxically simple for us to come to Him. He already paid the price on Calvary.

It is easy in that all it requires is faith and obedience. It is also difficult because it means the relinquishment of pride and the mentality that, "I can manage on my own." We have to surrender our very lives to God. Romans 10:9 promises, "that if you confess with your mouth the Lord Jesus and believe in your heart that God has raised Him from the dead, you will be saved."

The recipe for the life of a Christian is not burdened with endless commandments and orders. God tells us that His children demonstrate whose they are by their love for Him and by their love for others. We are told, "You shall love the Lord your God with all your heart, with all your soul, and with all our mind. This is the first and great commandment. And the second is like it: You shall love your neighbor as yourself. On these two commandments hang all the Law and the Prophets," (Matthew 22:37b-40).

The book of First John urges us to live out our Christianity by loving others. He even goes so far as to say that if we don't have love for our brothers and sisters then we can't profess to love God. "He who does not love does not know God, for God is love," (1 John 4:8).

Throughout my illness I have been blessed numerous times by others who practice a profound Christianity. I call these individuals 'quiet saints' because they will never appear on the evening news. They are the Mother Theresas without any press coverage at all. They will never speak to large congregations.

These are the kind of people who demonstrate the transcendent values that Christianity really espouses – the charity, the love and the brotherhood. This lifestyle reaches beyond current situations and touches us so very deeply. My prayer is that my life can be patterned after the examples these people have shown me and that I will be content to live the life of a quiet saint.

Bonnie

Bonnie was one such woman who reached out to help me at a great price to her own well-being. I met her while in the hospital with kidney failure. She shared a room with me. Bonnie was terminally ill, and I saw her during several other shorter stays, as well. Each time she patiently underwent chemotherapy and awaited her imminent death.

Before I was transferred to the intensive care unit during my initial stay with Bonnie, I continually grew weaker and more unable to steady myself upon getting out of bed. One morning I awoke at approximately 2:00 a.m. and had to go to the restroom. I didn't feel at all confident that I could make the short trip without assistance.

I buzzed the nurses' station in the stillness of the night. I waited several minutes but no one came to help me. Finally, I carefully slid out of bed and groped my way to the restroom, clinging to the walls of room for support. From the restroom I once again buzzed my night nurse, but still received no response following a long wait.

I knew I would have to attempt to return to my bed by myself, although the jaunt across the room had taken its toll the first time. On my return trip I fell, catching my foot under the table beside my bed. I was too feeble to move either the table or my foot. I was trapped.

Bonnie awakened out of a sound sleep when I stumbled. She immediately turned to face me, and used the side-rail of her bed to pull herself up to assist me. She somehow managed, amidst her tubes and wires, to prop herself up enough to scoot the table out of my way.

Not yet finished, Bonnie then extended an arm and allowed me to hoist myself up and back into the comforts of my bed. I watched in silent admiration as she then painfully groped to get back into her own bed.

I have thought many times about her compassion. No one was there to applaud her act of kindness. No one but me witnessed her unselfishness. I am quite certain that her assistance caused her a great deal of pain and I don't know what price may have been potentially paid with her health. But she never paused to give it a second thought that night. She just saw that I needed help, and gave me everything she had.

I met Bonnie's husband, Dana, also. He faithfully came each day to bide away the fleeting hours with his dying wife. They were truly amazing to watch as they faced the future with confidence and prayer. Bonnie was never quite well enough to attend the Catholic masses offered on the first floor of the hospital each Sunday morning. But Dana was always there, offering up his praise to God.

One particular Sunday morning I felt stronger than usual and really began to miss the fellowship of other worshippers. Dana had already burst into our room like a pleasant breeze from the outside world. He kindly invited me to attend mass with him. I panicked for just a moment. This was going to be a Catholic service. I was unfamiliar with the formalities of a mass, with the printed prayers. Dana, sensing my uncertainty, assured me with his friendly eyes that he would not abandon me.

He ushered me into a wheelchair, kissed Bonnie a temporary goodbye and off we went. I don't remember many details of the service. But I will always remember Dana, leaning over beside me with his little black book of prayers, quietly pointing to what came next. I came from that little chapel having really worshipped that morning because a man whom I barely knew, whose wife lay dying in the bed upstairs beside mine, took the time and effort to share his worship with me.

Tears still come to my eyes when I think about the unselfishness of this couple. I compare it to the story in Luke of the widow who gave two mites. The custom for the giving of tithes and offerings in Biblical times was to put money into the temple treasury upon entering the building.

One day a widow walked by and placed two small copper coins into the box. Many richer people were around her, giving much more in terms of monetary value. But Jesus said, "Truly I say to you that this poor widow has put in more than all; for all these out of their abundance have put in offerings for God, but she out of her poverty has put in all the livelihood that she had," (Luke 21:3-4).

At a very basic level, Bonnie extended a compassion that cost a lot. Her husband, as well, exerted extra effort meekly and unobtrusively. That is what Christianity is all about. It is simple to practice a Christianity that costs nothing. But there are times when we are called upon to give everything – and that is what Bonnie did for me.

I learned later from a nurse who knew us both that Bonnie had died. I experienced mixed emotions upon hearing the news. I would miss my friend and hospital roommate. But I also realized that her suffering was finally over. And I took comfort in the fact that Dana had a firm faith in God, Whom he would look to for solace to get him through.

Sister Martha

I can't write about quiet saints without thinking of Sister Martha, too. She was the director of the hospital's volunteer services, who countless times went beyond the call of duty for me. She was genuinely interested in my condition and always took my feeble hand in hers for a heartfelt prayer before ending a visit.

I don't remember when I first met Sister Martha but the majority of our time together was during my stay with meningitis. When I grew a bit stronger she began to extend her visits. They then included rides in my wheelchair up and down the halls and even outside, either sitting on a bench or in the picturesque hospital garden.

I'm sure some of those early visits must have been especially frustrating for her because no sooner would we get started toward our destination than I would be tired and ask to return to my bed. But Sister Martha never complained or acted as if I was a bother.

She fulfilled one of the chief tests of what a Christian is all about – unconditional love for another. I didn't get to know her as well as I would have liked. In retrospect, I can see that she got to know me very well indeed. She spent precious hours listening to my anger and frustration, and helped me explore the depths of my depression.

Sister Martha never preached to me. She never attempted to convert me to Catholicism. That wasn't why she was there. God placed her there to love me and to show me that real Christianity is a quiet, humble, powerful tool. Love and compassion are truly far superior to all the flamboyant sermons in the universe.

A Gentle Man

Finally, another person comes to mind when I think of quiet saints – an unassuming man I encountered while giving a devotional at church. That particular Sunday morning I spoke frankly about my condition and how I was learning to lean on the Lord through all the various trials, including my financial difficulties. I had just been forced to quit my job at McDonald's because of my extended illness and really had no income at all to pay for my graduate level tuition.

Following my talk, a man approached me quietly and alone. He said he firmly felt that the Lord had directed him to help someone out of his own financial blessings. God let him know while I was still speaking that I was that person.

He insisted that I accept a small sum from him every month throughout the duration of my schooling for my master's degree. There were two conditions: I must tell no one who he was, and I must promise to do the same for someone else in the future.

I was initially hesitant to take "charity." But I realized that if I really mean what I claim about Christian love and sharing, I have to be willing to allow others to help me when I am down. I must not get in the way. God was reaching out to me through his man.

I gratefully accepted the man's gift and he assisted me for several long months during a very critical financial time. I do not print his name because he would not wish me to do so. But I want to include this example of quiet sainthood because to me he demonstrated humble, selfless giving. He never asked for anything in return, not even a thank you.

There are many other selfless acts I could recount. But this sampling personifies for me the very nature and purpose of Christianity. These people, perhaps even without recognizing it, have helped me to grow and to strongly desire to be able to demonstrate a love for others that echoes God's love for all of us.

People like this give us glimpses into how the world is really supposed to be. Individuals such as these tear little holes in the fabric that separates us from the true world beyond us and allow cascades of light to shine through. When we bask in that light for even a short time, we realize how much better what is to come must be.

Chapter Sixteen:

Sharing the Burden

In my ongoing struggle to keep the lupus in remission so I could get on with my life, there have always been close friends and family ready to help care for me at a moment's notice. Mom and Dad desperately wanted to be able to protect me from further battles with my disease.

Mom became very protective, afraid I would take on too much at one time, fearful that yet another crisis would follow. At times I viewed this shielding as stifling because it reminded me of my fragility. I had to remember that she had seen me at my worst – at a time when I could recall little more than the fog of medication and pain.

The summer I was ensnared at home attempting to fully recuperate from the meningitis brought more offers of assistance. My sister, Karen, graciously insisted that she forfeit her impending plans for a move away from Nevada to take care of me.

She was able to hook me up to the I.V. when Mom was at work since I still didn't have my full vision back yet. She had memorized long before I did which of my twenty-seven pills I was to take, when and with what.

I was grateful for Karen's selfless offer and in the early stages of my homecoming I came to depend on her probably more than I should have. At the same time I harbored an appreciable amount of impending guilt.

I knew it was unfair to let her stay all summer with me. We both had our own lives to lead. She had just graduated from college and had her own dreams to chase. It wasn't right.

In the end, her move accomplished two things. It kept her from feeling trapped at home when she honestly felt she should be someplace else. It also forced me to gradually take more responsibility for myself. This increased my diminished level of independence. It made me ultimately feel better about myself just to be fully aware of my recommended medication dosages, something I had been putting off.

Feeling Lonely

Eventually I was able to work again and moved into one of my parents' rental houses. I had to be content to garner my self-reliance in stages. But what I really wanted was to find someone with whom I could share my life. As time went on I became increasingly skeptical that this would ever happen. After all, I reasoned, I had lost boyfriends in the past – some directly due to my illness.

Joe, the guy I had almost made the mistake of marrying, once informed me, "Jennie, if you plan to get sick in the near future, let me know now. I mean, if you expect me to drive all the way to the hospital to see you, I've got to work it into my schedule. Otherwise, with no advance notice, you can just forget it!"

Surely not all men could be so cold-hearted as to honestly think I planned my sicknesses. Yet who could I find that would be willing to share the burden of my lupus with all its uncertainties?

In my impatience I once more found myself unwilling to wait upon the Lord. In a prolonged state of what I refer to as my own personal "pity trip," I envisioned a lonely future and almost totally convinced myself that there was no one for me. Still I found myself begging God for a miracle.

I prayed specifically for two things. I wanted God to send me someone who was willing to accept me for who I was; lupus and all. I also fervently prayed that when I met him, God would let me know. I didn't want any doubts or to be so plagued by loneliness that I would accept less than God's ideal for me. This time I had to be sure.

I met Mike through Becky and Billy, my friends from the college speech and debate squad. Mike, Becky's cousin, lived in Joplin, Missouri, about an hour's drive from Nevada. Becky and Billy both knew I was lonely and offered to introduce me to Mike when they were home from graduate school for Christmas break in December of 1987.

Our first meeting was a double date. Then Becky invited me to attend a family New Year's Eve party the following weekend. The night of the party I watched Mike. I listened, laughed and had a superb time. When I climbed the stairs of Becky's house to sleep the rest of the night away, a strange sense of peace rolled over my entire body, enveloping me completely. I knew that night that I would marry Mike.

It wasn't until the end of January that we actually began dating. But our first real date was like magic. It was only a short time before we both knew we were in love. We began planning a life together.

Questioning God's Answer

I don't know why it is that we pray for something, have faith that God will answer and then question it when we finally are granted our desires. I never had any doubts that Mike and I were meant for each other.

But now that our relationship had taken a serious turn I became fearful that he was holding out on me, not sharing his true feelings about my chronic illness. He seemed too good to be true.

I had been diagnosed with my lupus almost five years before. I had gone through the stages of the grieving process – more than once. Yet now that I found myself about to commit to share the rest of my life with someone, I discovered that I began re-experiencing the stages.

I told myself it was for Mike's sake. Suddenly it didn't seem fair that someone who loved me so much should have to endure all the uncertainties of my disease. I felt apologetic and responsible for my frailty, as if it were somehow my fault.

When God introduced the institution of marriage in the Garden of Eden, Adam responded to the gift of Eve with a solemn declaration: "'This is now bone of my bones and flesh of my flesh; She shall be called Woman, because she was taken out of Man.'"

The Bible goes on to elaborate by saying, "Therefore a man shall leave his father and mother and be joined to his wife, and they shall become one flesh," (Genesis 2:23, 24). I knew that if Mike married me, we would be an integral, inseparable part of each other.

Looking back now, I see that Mike was actually prepared to share my physical weaknesses before I was really willing to let him. I knew I needed to be completely honest about the potential dangers involved with my disease, and I was. In reality I probably painted a worse picture than necessary. But I had to be certain that he was familiar with the risks and was willing to take them.

Mike's own father had died of a heart attack when Mike was only ten years old. He had experienced this significant loss before he met me. He had also seen his parents happily married for thirteen years. My own private fears were eased when Mike told me, "Jennie, I'd rather have thirteen good years than forty unhappy ones."

So Mike wanted me for who I was, not even considering whether or not I had a chronic illness. He didn't feel as if he was "settling" for less than what he hoped he would find. I just beamed.

I discovered in time that if God meant for me to cope with my lupus and if He meant for me to marry Mike, then He meant for us to deal with it together. I had to be reminded that I am not relying on my own strength or merit for my relationship. My plea for a healthy body for Mike's sake was only a reflection of selfishness on my part.

After all, God had taught me so very much through the course of my illness. How could I deny Mike the opportunity to grow and learn through my pain if God willed it?

Learning to Feel Secure

Another concern that was difficult to let go of was that of convincing myself that I indeed had something to contribute to the relationship. My medical expenses just for maintenance of the disease are excessive.

There was no guarantee of continued remission or that I would always be able to work, especially full time. I had been managing on my own for a time. Was it fair to shoulder someone else with this burden?

Mike brought so much into our marriage. Besides being able to provide financially, Mike had the enduring qualities of love, support and strength from which I could draw. What did I have?

God had to bring me back to a verse from the Sermon on the Mount before I was able to go any further. "But seek first the kingdom of God and His righteousness, and all these things shall be added to you," (Matthew 6:33).

I realized I could not depend upon either Mike or myself to provide for our physical requirements. God will make provisions for all our needs – if we first seek His will.

God has also shown me that my illness doesn't define who I am. I bring my own strengths into our marriage – my ability to listen and develop ideas, my willingness to serve others and my desire to keep God first in our lives. Every day I pray that God will help me be the kind of wife He would have me be; and every day I thank God for bringing us together.

Our greatest scare, prior to even getting officially engaged, occurred when we were playing softball with my church youth group one summer evening in 1988. Suddenly my Omaiah Reservoir began throbbing. It had been inserted into my head over two years before and I had never had a problem like this. I told Mike that something was very wrong. He held me as I cried, both of us anticipating the worst.

Without hesitation he agreed to skip work the next day and accompany me to my rheumatologist in Kansas City. He

160

also assured me, "Jennie, if you do have to go into the hospital, I will come and see you as often as I can. But I might not be able to make it every day."

He was talking about a drive of over 150 miles one way. I managed a slight smile. What he was really saying was that he would be there for me unconditionally. What a guy.

Initially I was informed that either the reservoir had somehow gotten infected and would have to be removed, which meant major surgery, or the meningitis had returned. While we waited in agony for the infectious disease doctor to confirm the report, Mike just kept a tight grip on my hand in the waiting room. The minutes seemed like hours.

Eventually we learned, much to our relief that the intense throbbing had actually been caused by a fluid build-up near the reservoir. No one knew just what had precipitated it.

Thankfully, simply inserting a needle into the reservoir and withdrawing the excess fluid solved the problem. If I ever had any doubts about Mike being by my side during a crisis, they melted away after this.

Mike has learned to read me very well. He knows when I am tired and brings me home early from outings with friends when necessary. He has become educated about my medical situation.

We also have an agreement borne out of my previous tendency to mask symptoms: he depends on me to be completely honest. If I need to go to a doctor or to the hospital, or if I need him for anything, I tell him. I have learned, through our arrangement, to put a great deal of denial behind me. We don't play games with my illness, and that is comforting.

Refocusing the Relationship

A potential difficulty among couples when one has a chronic illness is that the disease itself can become the focus of the relationship. The illness shouldn't dominate every conversation or be the exclusive factor in determining mutual or personal decisions. We are learning to lead balanced lives and to see beyond the sickness.

It isn't always easy because my disease isn't something I can ever completely separate myself from. It is always lurking in the background, ready to rear its ugly head at what I deem the most inopportune times. I cope with this by trying not to allow my sickness to overshadow his at times when he isn't feeling well.

I take an interest in his likes and hobbies, as he does in mine. We simply devote our time and attention to activities we enjoy. There is too little time for any of us to spend it dwelling on our frailties rather than basking in the pleasures God has given us. This attitude keeps us mentally and emotionally healthy.

As with any relationship, Mike and I both bring our strengths as well as our vulnerabilities. Being with Mike is teaching me to be more aware of who I am as a person, and who I want to become.

Before I could commit to the marriage I had to be humbled to the point where I was willing to be closely interdependent with someone else. I had to be ready for the fact that whatever happened to me was going to happen to us as a couple. As I alluded to earlier, that diminished my need for the denial stage.

I have prayed since I was quite young that God would prepare me for the proper mate, and he for me. Part of accepting God's answer to that prayer involved trusting that He had prepared Mike to marry someone in my condition. It also included a willingness to let Mike truly share the burden.

I have come to the point where I can honestly thank God for my health problems because of what Mike is learning and how he is being given the opportunity to grow. In the meantime, I praise God for my husband and for his willingness to share my burden.

Chapter Seventeen:

Choices

Although we know differently, we like to think of ourselves as imperishable, sometimes paying only passing lip service to our own mortality. It isn't uncommon for us to be uncomfortable around hospitals and cemeteries. They are material manifestations, reminding us that death is real and not so very far away. The stark reality of death scoffs at our feeble natures and underscores our vulnerabilities.

We are consciously aware that ours is merely one of countless generations that have brought their era's hopes and dreams to a climax. But like the generations that have preceded us, often our personal aspirations are only to be lost in the dust of the decades that will follow. At its best, our art and literature remind us of our own mortality.

Our cultural endeavors suggest our limitations and ultimately communicate the larger message that death is the final arbiter of our disputes. Even ecologists constantly warn us that we only have the world on loan from future generations.

It is highly unlikely that any of us confront death until it confronts us, or someone close to us. I know this was certainly true for me. Only when I came face to face with the reality of my own mortality did I truly begin to contemplate death on a personal level.

Twice I have been close to death. Twice the Lord has chosen to issue a reprieve – but not a complete healing. I realize that I am living on borrowed time.

I am not insinuating that we should constantly dwell on our impending transience. To do so would make us become narrow-minded in focus and render us counterproductive. But for me, the stark reality of my disease's potential to strip away my health or my life is never far removed. The knowledge of how close I have been to death and how quickly I could be in that position again hovers in the shadows of my mind, struggling to initiate a defeatist attitude.

Despair as the Easy Choice

Despair in the face of suffering is the easy out for any of us. Hopelessness is self-pitying and sustaining. The despair borne of depression is much easier because once we begin it is so simple to continue. It feeds on itself, looming ever deeper and darker.

Many people actually choose despair for these reasons. It gives them a sense of orientation. Despair affords us the opportunity to rail against the world, against basic unfairness, against God. We feel free to vent our frustrations impotently against the universe. But that is all it is – an ineffective, useless philosophy.

There is a sense of despair that can grip each of us, no matter how much or how little we might suffer in this world. If we are born, we live, we die, and that is all there really is, then truly despair seems the only viable option.

Indeed, life without hope is meaningless. If there really is nothing more than this life and this life is filled with pain, then existence itself is purposeless. Suffering of any kind does us absolutely no good. It accomplishes nothing.

French philosopher Blaise Pascal purported an argument that he referred to as a wager, literally a bet about God. He posited that if we believe in God and God does exist, then we receive an eternal reward. If we do not believe in God's existence and there truly is no God, then we are still all right.

If we believe in God and He doesn't exist, then we have only wasted our time, perhaps missed out on some "fun". However, if we refuse to believe God exists and He actually does, then we are eternally doomed.

If the so-called bet with God helps us begin to sort out our thoughts about the reality of God, fine. But merely winning a wager with God denies us the chance to experience a real, vital, personal relationship with Him. Knowing the Lord as much more than a Creator or an impersonal Figure had enabled me to choose something besides despair.

Hope as the Better Choice

That second choice is hope. Because I believe in Jesus Christ as my personal Lord and Savior, I know there is much more than just this life. Revelation 21:3-4 provides us with a picture of the world to come for those who believe:

> *And I heard a loud voice from heaven saying, "Behold, the tabernacle of God is with men, and He will dwell with them, and they shall be His people, and God Himself will be with them and be their God. And God will wipe away every tear from their eyes; there shall be no more death, nor sorrow, nor crying; and there shall be no more pain, for the former things have passed away."*

I rest assured that when my life on earth is ended I will be with God in heaven. That is the source of my ultimate hope. But hope on a daily basis in the midst of struggle is much more difficult to maintain. It fades.

Hope must be fed by the love and compassion from those around us. When our plight seems its bleakest we must rely on the assurance of Romans 8:28 that, "...all things work together for good to those who love God, to those who are the called according to His purpose."

Choosing Hope

I have lived with depression and despair, but I have chosen hope. There are still times when I am temporarily inconsolable but I always climb out of my despondency. Most of us don't have to look very far to see people who began a certain crisis filled with hope and strength but gradually succumbed to despair.

All the hope disappeared and they were left as shallow, pathetic shells of what they once were. I have to make a conscious daily effort to see that this doesn't happen to me.

Psychoanalyst Eric Fromm once posited that when we come to the end of our lives we will look back with despair if we view our lives as useless, meaningless and unfulfilled. However, we will look back with a sense of dignity if we are proud of our lives, and of what we have accomplished.

My goal is to live each day I am given to its very fullest. Sometimes I think of my time as having been prorated. I am learning to savor each moment, squeezing out the purposes and achievements I truly desire day by day. This is something we must all do. Without this effort and determination we will soon find our lives have passed us by and nothing meaningful has been done.

We can help others who are suffering by allowing them to see the hope that lives in us. If we profess to be Christians we have an even greater task. First Peter 3:15 instructs us:

"But sanctify the Lord God in your hearts, and always be ready to give a defense to everyone who asks you a reason for the hope that is in you, with meekness and fear." When others see the hope we carry with us through every crisis, then we can share the Source of that hope.

And so my life continues, with all its daily struggles sometimes more difficult than the major testing of hospitalizations and ominous bouts with death. I pray that the contents of this book will bring all of us to a deeper understanding of the God that can sustain us in any situation.

Epilogue:

From Then Till Now

Much time has transpired since I first began writing this book. I have learned much and pray that you have been blessed. My subsequent struggles with a kidney transplant and cancer have brought with them more lessons and an ever-deepening walk with my Savior. Expressing the story of these events, however, would deter from this book's primary purpose, and so are left to the next.

To all those who have read my story, I invite you to join me in claiming Paul's declaration as your own: "For I have learned in whatever state I am, to be content," (Philippians 4:11b).

About the Author

Jennie Martin earned her M.S. in Counseling Psychology, in addition to her B.A. in speech and psychology. She is currently a Licensed Professional Counselor working with individuals, couples and families. After suffering renal failure due to systemic lupus, Jennie received a kidney transplant from her brother. She is now cancer free, after surviving major surgery for stage three cancer and its previous recurrences. She and her husband make their home in Farmington, Arkansas where they are active in their local church.

www.ingramcontent.com/pod-product-compliance
Lightning Source LLC
Chambersburg PA
CBHW050122280326
41933CB00010B/1201